Flying with the Storks

Volume 5

Flying with the Storks

Volume 5
by Dimitris Zorbas

MYTHOS
PRESS

2022

Flying with the Storks
Volume 5

Copyright © 2022 by Dimitris Zorbas

Cover by: D. Zorbas

All rights reserved.
No part of this book may be reproduced in any form, except for brief reviews, without written permission from the author.

First edition
First printing

ISBN-13: 978-0-9889314-2-8

Published by Mythos Press
Post Office Box 566
Plymouth, California 95669

Printed in the United States of America

Contents

Chapter 1.   Flying West   1
Chapter 2.   West to East   67

Chapter 1. Flying West

1.01

It has been raining in earnest for three days with more rain forecast for today. We prepare for the trip to India and Bhutan with some apprehension because of our unfamiliarity with the culture, our ignorance of history and customs. I hope that the gratification from the natural beauty of the journey will counterbalance any cultural shock we might experience.

At the change of seasons a pessimistic mood has seized me due to the absence of luminous days. Early winter depresses me. *Il pleut dans mon cœur comme il pleut sur la ville...*I was born under the sunlight of Greece and remain its worshipper.

Fiddletown 3 November 2008

1.02

Finally it is daylight at the Sacramento Airport as we wait to board United Express to San Francisco which leaves one half hour later than the itinerary indicated. The evening was spent at the Primrose condo where the news of Barak Obama's victory reached us, making us hopeful again for this country, in spite of the formidable obstacles that lie ahead.

I think of Alexia at the farm, spending her days waiting for our appearance vainly. I think of our home lacking our presence and sounds, silently waiting in the turning weather and our car UBP parked in an open stall at Primrose because of pending carport work.

After an entire year of commitment, planning and waiting, time has come for the India-Bhutan visit, which by now seems an impulsive move. They are countries in a region of the world where we feel entirely uninformed and which we have to approach carefully and openly as outside observers.

An airline ground-attendant inquires for our San Francisco flight's final destination.

- Delhi, I answer, thinking how strange the response sounds...

Sacramento 11/04/2008

For a third time this year we find ourselves in SFO queuing up at the security check-up area of the International Terminal. Here is a gateway to the East thanks to services of airlines the likes of ANA, Cathay Pacific, JAL, Thailand Airlines and a few others.

On the way to the departure gate a stop for coffee and snack (small brioche-dough croissants) at double the cost than at any good San Francisco shop charges. We swallow the anti-malarial pills that rightfully ought to have had a quinine taste to match the price paid at the airport shop.

Down one level we sit down at the A6 Gate area where a large group of impeccably dressed young and pretty Chinese attendants gather for the flight. The passengers trickle in, Chinese, Americans, an Indian family and some Koreans. We wait with everyone for boarding the large aircraft being made ready in the clear autumnal light of a beautiful day in the Bay Area.

SFO 4 November 2008

The Hong Kong airport is spacious, new and emanates an aura of friendliness. After a fifteen plus hours flight from San Francisco it is a welcome respite even though we would have preferred to have reached the final destination, but the flight for Delhi does not leave till after 22:10 arriving at Delhi at 02:00 tomorrow morning. I now wonder about the decision to arrange for a city tour the same day.

In flight we slept fitfully in segments, watched mindlessly silly movies and the progress of the flight. The service was inconsistent, even peculiar at times and the food did not rise above mediocre, typical airline fare. Cathay Pacific, although it has left me unimpressed, offers service superior to American carriers.

On board Cathay Pacific 6 November 2008

* *1.03*

Arriving to Delhi's Indira Gandhi International Airport it was as if a gate to the Third World opened wide in front of our eyes. Even though this is the major hub of this region it suffers from lack of maintenance and renovation. As soon as we enter a chaotic lower level to claim the luggage, the haze visible from the airplane seems to fill all space depositing a film of dust on every surface. Fifteen minutes after Elaine retrieved the first suitcase, getting a bad leg bruise, we retrieve the second piece of luggage from the conveyor belt with the flight's last luggage batch. We exit in the hall where many drivers are waiting for incoming passengers, each brandishing name signs. Accidentally my eye catches a placard with my name held by a small dark and saturnine man who taking a hold of the larger suitcase marches on resolutely for five minutes through the crowd, with us in tow, to the parking area where the air is thick with wood burning smoke. Quickly placing the luggage in the boot of a small car he opens the rear door for us to sit in and takes off through a stony path leading to two parking area exit toll-booths. Inside the booths sit men in gray shirts with rolled up sleeves gravely counting toll money. It is past two thirty in the morning yet for those shadows life moves in narrow spaces that broken glass panes reconnect with the outside world. As we leave the airport we see many signs of feverish construction which we assume to be a general expansion of the operations.

The car bounces on potholes and uneven paving while it changes directions and streets. I look for signs of a revitalized city but what I see is thick haze, dusty foliage and unmaintained structures, all trying to avoid unseemly attention. My mood grows bleak while I reconsider a misplaced belief in the state of India. At the hotel the feeling worsens when the driver demands money for the fare the hotel will be charging us. This becomes the first of a series of episodes in dealing with the people here.

In the ill-kempt room we arrange our things and lie down at the pre-dawn hour to sleep, troubled by the uncertainty of tomorrow.

....
The ring from the alarm clock takes me by surprise, I apparently have fallen asleep. In the bathroom I test the shower and find it to work enough for our needs. I brush my teeth with sterilized water and we make ready for breakfast at the terrace swathed in the din and pollution of traffic which grinds to a halt in the outer loop of Connaught Circus. Another time with clear skies and fewer cars perhaps this could have been a lovely place.
....
How did we get so mixed up in this infernal machine of making-do business Indian-style? Everyone claims to be associated one way or another with the Indian Government, which on the other hand makes no effort to safeguard its own good name allowing anyone to come up with schemes to fleece unaware tourists. Through the affable operator we meet at the hotel, who only later find out is in the travel business, we buy the package he sells for Agra and later he manages to get another cut from our purchases at a store presenting itself as the Government sponsored cottage industry. And all through this our day driver Anil takes us to the most important Delhi sites. He is a little more polished and a little less greedy, though perhaps an oversized tip he receives from us may have pushed him over.

A jumble of images, impressions, unexpected encounters, all wrapped in the warm brown haze of dust, particulate pollution and fog. The driver Anil, who arrives at the appointed time, drives us to Old Delhi to put us on a Pedi cab. The tiny man who pedals hard pulling the weight of two people in and out of impossible traffic carries us to Jama Masjid first. The entrance to the mosque stairs on which we must leave our shoes where clean is a relative word and helpfulness a ruse to demand money. This is a bad start of a long day. The little Moslem man waits at his Pedi cab to transport us to the Red Fort where long lines of people wait for the security agents to clear them for the visit. Once inside the size of the fort overwhelms you but it is the number of people that engulf and asphyxiate us.

From the Red Fort to lunch, where Westerners go, a place Anil knows. He waits outside or someplace, where we know the car is parked somewhere jammed in and cannot be moved out easily.

Raj Ghat is part of a large complex of Parks, a place to walk in sunlight and pay respects to Mahatma Gandhi. On a bench we rest on, we are approached by two young women, curious and attracted to Elaine. I take their photo, they laugh, they chatter both in English and Hindi. The day grows long and before it is over we would like to visit Humayun's Tomb, a serene like park place that is worth more than given credit. Here we have a preview of Taj Mahal. The red sun is too weak to bring out important details of many buildings, it is close to setting. Anil finally drives us back by way of Delhi Gate.

....

In the hotel room we drink tea and have toast after the review of our foolish behavior today, mulling tomorrow and the day after when our trip to the Ancient Buddhist Kingdoms begins.

I am deeply disappointed with our experience in Delhi, both because of the human aspect and of the heavy air pollution. To India's heat and dust a third plague has been added, smog.

Delhi 7 November 2008

* *1.04*

We both collapse in bed at past eleven P.M. to sleep after our return from an all-day exhausting trip to Agra. Will I dream of Taj Mahal without rancor tonight? I doubt it as I doubt I will dream of Agra at all...

Delhi 8 November 2008

* *1.05*

In the relative orderliness of the Domestic Airport while we wait at the lounge of Jet Airways for the departure of our flight I use the brief respite for recording my impressions. Finally we escape from the curse of air pollution in this part of India, hoping to be soon in cooler and mountainous places where one can breathe freely clean air.

....
SATURDAY NIGHT LIVE IN DELHI...

The Agra trip was very disappointing though with some redeeming aspects. At a few minutes before 08:00 the front desk notifies us that our driver has arrived. We have just finished breakfast on the veranda upstairs wrapped in the cool smoky haze of the early morning. You can almost feel the grit in your lungs. It is a pity for such a beautiful place to be so badly blighted.

Downstairs we are expected by the driver introduced as Manuch and another passenger in a small car instead of the van we anticipated. The driver is pleasant; his English is fluent and appears to be a forward person. Our co-passenger introduces herself as Andrea; she is a young businesswoman from Colombia who has founded a company facilitating exports of Chinese manufacturers to other parts of the world.

Driving is stressful to me but Manuch keeps calm and very alert constantly honking, breaking, accelerating and avoiding collisions. At the outskirts of the city he stops for some paperwork. I step out to buy a bottle of water at a little roadside store, paying with a 100 Rs note. The fellow gives me back a handful of notes none of which are Indian and at my refusal to accept them tries to pawn off all sorts of other currencies, until he finally relents to give me change in local currency. Meanwhile the car has been besieged by monkeys, a man with a cobra and an assortment of kids who try to extract money from the passengers.

- Sir, says the man with a young cobra in small basket, would you not be buying my cobra? Only 100 Rs sir, and extends the basket to me.

....
Iskandra (Alexandria) is the location of great Mughal emperor Akbar's tomb by the road to Agra. I reflect of the passing centuries, names left behind when flesh is dust and empires only a name. Alexander is well and ruling forever in the mythical world of barbaric language.

....
The Agra Fort, red as well, is enormous and impressive. Crowds line up to enter; foreign visitors have to pay an ever increasing entrance fee. Spectacular ramparts that probably never faced a formidable enemy look down upon the inner space with many outsized buildings. From a balustrade facing Taj Mahal we hardly discern its outline in the thick gray haze.

....
How can I fall again for a ruse? Easily, as it turns out when I follow the "gardener" who has "an eye for photography" and shuttles me to improbable places to capture Taj Mahal's waning reflected light. In the end he shows his hand when he demands some compensation with a straight face. I am furious with myself; I become mad enough not to allow myself to fall victim of another con artist. The time is short, we rush to the point we are supposed to find Andrea but she is not there. We wait while waves of people are disgorged through the inner gate, without end it seems, but no Andrea. Ultimately we decide to check with Manuch by returning to the parked car, when fortuitously we meet Andrea at the outer gate. Relieved we return together to start an interminable return drive of more than four hours to Delhi.

....
We sleep briefly and rise early to pack and get ready for the flight to Bagdogra. The taxi drops us off to the Domestic Airport which is in better repair than the International.

Delhi Domestic Airport 9 November 2008

* 1.06

Day 1: Bagdogra to Darjeeling. (Nov 09) We transfer from Bagdogra Airport to Darjeeling by jeep or Mini Coach. The drive is three to four hours through tea gardens, villages, and towns and at times runs near the tracks of the toy train that goes to Darjeeling. We will stay two nights in Darjeeling.

* 1.07

Driving to Delhi Domestic Airport we pass through large green park areas and upscale neighborhoods where each multi-family building appears to have controlled access by private security guards, while others defend themselves behind formidable walls with razor barbed wire and glass shards. Over everything the particulate air pollution has applied a coat of gray-yellow soot.

At the airport we check in at the Jet Airways counter and wait for the flight to Bagdogra. The service is impeccable and the lunch unexpectedly good though I have little time to enjoy it because I become involved in a conversation with the traveler seated next to me.

Andy was an undergraduate at Caltech in the 1970s studying Chemical Engineering. Now in Pittsburgh he is married to an Indian woman and member of the faculty at the University. His destination is a remote place in Sikkim where a world conference of Chemical Engineers is convened for the third time. We talk about India, Caltech, science and the state of the world. All too soon the plane is landing at Bagdogra Airport in Siliguri. We retrieve the luggage and wait for John Bird and the other group members to show up.

....

The incomplete group in the small bus gets to know each other while speeding toward the Himalayan foothills and I find that John Bird fits my initial impression. The skies are blue again but haze and pollution persist. The bus weaves in and out of low hills and finally starts climbing cutting through verdant slopes.

Flying West

During a short stop at a restaurant we have a cup of tea and the first glance of the Himalaya snow-capped range.

....

At night we arrive at the Himalayan Resort perched at one of the steep streets in Darjeeling and check in. Dinner awaits us with instructions for a very early rising. The food is very good, our eyelids heavy and time precious. John Bird gets a birthday cake for turning 70.

.Darjeeling, Gorkaland 9 November 2008

1.08

Day 2: (Nov 10) We start well before dawn on an excursion to Tiger Hill for sunrise views of Kanchenjunga, the third highest peak in the world at 27,943 ft. We will also visit the Ghoom Monastery. After breakfast we take a half-day city tour of Darjeeling that includes visiting a tea estate, the Tibetan Refugee Self Help Center, Himalayan Mountaineering Institute, and the zoo. After lunch we take the fabled toy train ride to Ghoom and return to the hotel by jeep.

A long day ends on a good note after retrieving my lost camera case with the equipment at the Buddhist Monastery visited earlier in the morning. An entire day packed with events started at 03:15 to get an early start to Tiger Point for watching the sunrise over the Himalaya range.

....

After a cup of tea we board the Range Rovers and head to Tiger Hill in the pre-dawn darkness. On the way we encounter many other vehicles driving in the same direction and little children walking to school. We were told that the reason for rising up so early is to get there before the other tourists that had the same idea, though as soon as we drive up Tiger Hill we know we are the late comers. The walk up the hill is aided with little flashlights and starlight. Masses on the hilltop await the sunrise and have occupied all the choice places. More and more people keep pouring in, mostly Indians. Enterprising locals go around peddling hot coffee or panoramic photos of the mountain range. The cold is getting sharper while we stand around waiting impatiently for dawn to break. Photoflashes go off regularly and the noise level keeps rising. Finally a pale lavender glow announces the end of darkness revealing gradually the gray ghosts of the snowcapped Kanchendzonga. How many photos are being snapped each second, I wonder each time I press the camera button.

Gradually the crowds begin to thin as the light of day reveals the stark beauty of the snowcapped peaks. The ground on Tiger Hill is littered with paper and plastic. Shall we organize a clean-up party for the refuse the Zoroastrian disciples have left behind? Instead tired and hungry we return to the hotel for breakfast.

....

The Rovers transport us to the Ghoom Yiga Choling Buddhist Monastery, our first in this trip. At the end of the street a colorful gate leads to a parking area with a bad-weather shelter for visitors using public transportation. The temple is decorated with Buddhist symbols and figures painted in vivid colors. An array of bronze prayer wheels is positioned for the visitor to spin during entrance and exit. In the antechamber two large wheels with bells require more than a single person to set them in full motion. Inside a lama stands by a table surrounded by two large copper lamps that cause the suspended above prayer wheels to turn. He collects the money for use of cameras inside. We take the shoes off to enter while Rajiv proceeds to explain details of the temple and to present a historical brief. We put on our shoes, linger a little longer then we board the vehicles to return to the hotel.

Before we assemble for lunch I realize that I have misplaced the camera bag and begin to search for it in vain. We agree that I must have left it at the Ghoom Monastery and enlist help from the hotel and Rajiv. With the anxiety over a potential loss I do not enjoy the lunch that is one of the better to-date.

The Toy Train to Ghoom leaves in half hour, we board it and wait. The train whistles and begins to move spewing thick smoke and fine water mist; it winds its way through town, surprising shop owners and customers alike who happen to stand at the entrance of tiny shops. There is a stop at a colorful garden with a medicinal herb garden where Elaine notes the presence of cannabis in the printed catalog. Still riddled with anxiety we arrive at the train station at Ghoom where we disembark. Rajiv, Elaine and I climb on one of the vehicles that take us to the monastery. The doors are half closed, Rajiv calls out to the lama and from the interchange I guess they had found the bag which now the lama brings from the back of the temple. Overjoyed I thank them, climb back to the vehicle and we are on our way to join the others.

....

The tea plantation is located outside of Darjeeling at a much lower elevation which is accessed by a steep hairpin narrow road the vehicles negotiate.

In the way we encounter children walking home after a day of school. Further down we find ourselves surrounded by short bushes of *camellia sinensis* planted in terraced hills. When we enter the courtyard of the plantation we find ourselves facing several buildings for converting camellia leaves to marketable tea. Rajiv leads a tour of the facilities explaining the processes and machinery involved. On the third floor of a building suffused with strong floral aroma we see long vented trays where tea leaves are dried with the help of large turbines forcing air through. In an adjoining building the final processing and packaging of the tea takes place. Unmistakable and alluring scent of the processed leaves fills our nostrils. As we board the Rovers again a great swarm of schoolchildren comes upon us noisy and gregarious, easily smiling, waving or posing for photos.

The last visit of the day takes us to the Tibetan Refugee Self Help Center where the Darjeeling Tibetan community tries to maintain its identity having established a nucleus of handicraft workshops to preserve tradition and self-sufficiency. We watch and photograph people at work, young girls, women, old men and children without confines, moving through the entire space. As I look at the young I am convinced they will assimilate in the society at large that their community lives in.

....
At dinner we celebrate Rudy's 73 with a cake again.

Darjeeling, Gorkaland 10 November 2008

1.09

Day 3: (Nov 11) Transfer from Darjeeling to Pemayangtse. Our drive from Darjeeling to Pemayangtse will take six to seven hours, passing through traditional Sikkimese Villages, rich green forests, and cardamom plantations.

The bus parked by the entrance, luggage being unloaded and the travel group in the lawn area of the Tashigang Resort at Yangtey near Pelling, Sikkim, relishes a cup of tea. In one of those rare moments in life I catch a view of Kanchendzonga surrounded by clouds in solemnity and staring sternly back. It is hard remembering what season is when trilling cicadas, blooming poinsettias, hibiscus and fruit trees, speak of summer.

....
I rise at 05:00 with roosters crowing, surprised to see daylight when I pull the curtains open. The program calls for a seven hour ride to Pelling in Sikkim with short stops for refreshments and box lunch.

Last evening in Darjeeling, we had a respite long enough to take a shower and pack most of our things. Yet when we arrived to our room after the eventful day we discovered the water and the heater did not operate. This turned out to be an electrical problem that took some time to fix. We managed to take a shower, albeit a cold one for me and to heat a little the cold room. After dinner we put a few more things together and Elaine applied ice to her swollen ankle before getting exhausted to bed by 22:00. We slept soundly even with repeated interruptions from barking dogs.

The breakfast, brief and hurried takes place as the luggage is loaded to a little bus. Before departing JB thanks KK (the hotel owner) for the hospitality who in turn thanks the group and urges him and the rest to champion Darjeeling's needs to Sierra Club. Carrying personal items we board the bus starting the long drive. Through the town it is a struggle to advance in the maze of twisting lanes with oncoming traffic and all kinds of obstacles. After Ghoom we take a route that leads northwest, the vehicle running now on better paved roads. The lush vegetation changes as we descend in a valley. Temperate zone vegetation is replaced by a subtropical one as the Himalayan peaks hide behind a green wall.

We pass through villages, settlements and small towns, all with similar types of stores. People here like in the rest of the Darjeeling region have more Mongolian features than in Delhi and Punjab. Often I am misled to thinking that we are in some other South East Asian country. They are friendly though and perhaps more forward or less cunning than their brethren further south. School children wave, laugh and love to have their picture taken.

We are now almost at the level of a meandering whitewater river Rangit that becomes later part of Tika which runs to the sea by joining Ganges near Kolkata. Tall trees, including many teak trees are growing densely and in shadier areas are draped with fine moss.

Gradually the bus ascends anew; the air becomes cooler and slightly clearer. The sun is edging towards the mountainous horizon when we pull up to a resort hotel. The staff welcomes us with the familiar to us by now silk blessing scarf.

We wait for the luggage to unload on the lawn of a garden next to the main building. Sikkim tea is served for welcome. We soon become awed and entranced with the Himalayan range snowcapped peaks, soon the target for all cameras.

In the evening we are served a good mild Indian meal. We retire to prepare for tomorrow's trip.

Tashigang Resort, Sikkim 11 November 2008

1.10
Day 4: (Nov 12) Early morning visit to Pemayangtse Monastery, the second-oldest monastery in Sikkim, and return to hotel for breakfast. We then proceed to Gangtok, which will take six to seven hours driving through terraced farms, villages, and the famed Terri Tea Garden of Sikkim. We continue our drive to Gangtok where we stay two nights.

Much to everyone's regret, we must press on leaving behind us the lovely sanctuary of Tashigang Resort where we spent an evening in a room that faced the high Himalayan peaks and terraced rice farms. We eat our breakfast quietly before boarding the bus. We may have to return to the hotel for the box lunches that have not been prepared yet.

Over snaking mountain roads we cross little valleys and climb up to reach the Pemayangtse Monastery. The young students of the Buddhist Monastery are on a break watching us curiously or making themselves scarce. As we walk about the premises a sonorous bell begins to ring calling the students to class who respond obediently as a group except for a few laggards arriving late. We now can hear the chanting of sutras, the clear voice of the bell and the slow beat of sonorous wood plank. For a moment time stands still frozen like the distant high peak snows.

Off with shoes we enter the main prayer building, stepping on wood floors and stone or concrete surfaces. Rajiv leads the way explaining the contents, the images, the details of this Buddhist sect and you can see his smiling face animated, glowing. Up three floors in the *goemba* the air is thinner like a dream of counting moments as dew drops.

....

After a stop at a roadside café for an outdoor picnic lunch where we share our boiled eggs with an old mangy dog, we settle in the bus for a long ride through valleys and ridges, villages and rice farms, sunny spots and shady sides, to Gantok where we check in Hotel Nor-Khill. The hotel located at a high point of the city across from a large football stadium is luxurious with quirky inefficiencies and minor problems, though overall it seems as the most elegant of all places we have been so far. We are to stay here for two nights.

Dinner is as usual at 19:00 served in elegance. Gene, Elaine and I finish it off with a glass of local Sikkim brandy exhibiting full body and distinct nose.

Gantok, Sikkim 12 November 2008

1.11

Day 5: (Nov 13) Morning excursion to Rumtek Monastery, the Seat of his Holiness the Gyalwa Karmapas with its Nalanda University for teaching the Kargyu disciplines of Tibetan Buddhism. We return to our hotel via the Institute of Tibetology, which houses many antiquities from the collection of the King of Sikkim along with 3,000 volumes of Xylographs. After lunch, we enjoy sightseeing in Gangtok, visiting the Enchey Monastery, catching a flower show, and walking around the downtown bazaar.

In the morning we visit to the Rumtek Monastery, seat of Gyalwa Karmapas, which I find rather insipid in spite of its fine location.

The Institute of Tibetology is next in our itinerary. The building has several floors of which we find the ground floor to be the most interesting with its exhibits of old thangkas, statues and other items.

We return to the hotel for an excellent continental lunch.

Later in the afternoon we visit the Government Institute of Cottage Industries then we take a stroll at the market in Gantok where we buy gifts and finally tea both from Darjeeling and Sikkim.

The dinner served tonight is based on local cuisine though it is obviously toned down to suit Western palates.

Gantok, Sikkim 13 November 2008

* 1.12

Day 6: Gangtok to Kalimpong. (Nov 14) Our drive to Kalimpong will be mainly alongside the Testa River. After lunch and sightseeing in Kalimpong we will visit the Durpin Monastery, which is famous for the Mandala paintings on its ceilings and walls along with different deities of Tibetan Buddhism. We will also visit local flower nurseries and a market. This is a place to see village life.

The day begins badly. Elaine needs to have her ankle examined by a doctor. It is impossible to do that in Gantok without major delays. JB produces antibiotics for her to begin a precautionary treatment until we get to Kalimpong where a doctor can be visited.

After a short stop at the border of Sikkim for passport control, bathroom stop and a visit to the official but tiny handicrafts store the trip is resumed. Driving to Kalimpong takes around three hours negotiating a curvy road next to Testa River and farming country. Villages dot the landscape while the condition of the road makes it impractical to drive smoothly. Occasionally we run into groups of monkeys who seem undisturbed by traffic.

The hotel we are staying in Kalimpong, Silver Oaks, is in the center of town, elegant, at the top of a knoll and surrounded by beautiful gardens. The courtyard which is used as parking area is small and immediately adjacent to the narrow street, a challenge for parking anything, especially for larger vehicles.

A few minutes after our arrival Rajiv has arranged for the hotel's shuttle to transport Elaine, Rick who also needs medical attention, Gene, me and himself to the doctor with whom an appointment has been made.

Pharmacy in front, in the back an office for the physician, corridor for waiting patients, a procedure room and a nurse office, all tiny. Elaine's examination reveals infection necessitating lancing, cleaning of area, bandaging, tetanus shot and administration of antibiotic and anti-inflammatory. After nurse care, Elaine has to buy sandals for minimizing the pressure exercised on the leg. Rajiv brings us to a nearby shop where we buy locally produced footwear resembling a known brand.

Before the afternoon visit to Durpin Monastery and a flower nursery we sit down to a rushed lunch. Later free time to visit to town shops. I go along with David, Desiree, Cassandra, Marta and Rajiv who guides us to quality stores. Elaine remains at the hotel resting her injured leg. The market is pulsing with activity lending photo opportunities not always exploited. I find the last store's inventory interesting, especially its older pieces that I am particularly drawn to. Eventually I end up buying a few pieces.

We return to the hotel in darkness illuminated in the marketplace by the store lights, but as we draw further up near the hotel, soft and uncertain light gives everything an added dimension of past times. The students on hunger strike for Gorkaland smile as we go past their place at the edge of the market.

Dinner at 19:00 as usual gathers most of the group in the dining room. Still it is a short evening because of the planned early morning rising for tomorrow's a long trip.

Sometime later the hotel front desk calls everyone in the group to settle their bar bills because in the morning money transaction are not handled before 08:00. Lots of people are annoyed.

Kalimpong, W. Bengal 14 November 2008
✣

1.13

Day 7: Kailimpong to Phuntsholing. (Nov 15) We drive from Kalimpong to Phuntsholing, a town on the border between India and Bhutan where we spend the night.

The birds wake up at the same time as the alarm clock goes off. I look outside to see just darkness and it is only after I finish washing I see the light of dawn over the mountains. Elaine seems to be doing better. We pack everything and go down to have breakfast. The group is ready though the staff seems confused and breakfast takes longer than expected.

The trip starts a few minutes past seven, following a southeast route to Phuntsholing. The day is overcast, which probably helps to keep down the temperature. Elaine and Lori sit in the back seat with their legs elevated, exposed to the violent motion of the bus in bad sections of the road. I sit with John on the seat in front of them.

Gradually the hills become flatter and we find ourselves in the plains of India with tropical vegetation and different people, Bengalis, who look entirely different than their neighbors of the hills above. The plains grow rice, tea and other crops and host cattle, buffalo and goats. Poverty is extreme and lack of sanitation shocking.

The bus stops at a truck stop for (box) lunch. The place is relatively clean but only that. I refuse the use of a toilet preferring to wait until we reach our destination. The box lunch content is slightly different, sandwich with cheese (?), boiled egg, vegetable chicken patty, fries, cake and banana. It is nutritious and edible.

Finally after seven hours we reach Phuntsholing and go through the exit process from India. Less than one kilometer away is the gate to Bhutan. The bus pulls in the Hotel Druk parking. The staff of the hotel and the crew of the bus unload our luggage. It is time to say goodbyes to Rajiv, driver and driver helper. After so many days of traveling together we have come to consider them members of the group proper, particularly the cheerful, energetic, knowledgeable and always obliging Rajiv.

The Bhutan crew is not here yet; we check in our rooms and settle in. Druk has nothing to recommend it and in comparison to the previous places is distinctly inferior and run-down.

At the first floor veranda Lori and John, John Bird, Elaine and I sit to talk over drinks. Much of the discussion centers on Bhutan and India and their relations. John Bird gets a phone call from the next crew's guide who is downstairs.

We meet for dinner again; Indian choices tonight though with an added punch. The staff is neither friendly nor efficient, inattentive at times they seem to be fussing over trivial things and never have correct change. If in this country tipping were inappropriate before, now in this hotel it is endemic.

Desiree and Gene change Elaine's bandage before going to bed.

Phuntsholing, W. Bengal 15 November 2008
❖

1.14
_____

Day 8: Phuntsholing to Thimphu. (Nov 16) After our visas are processed, we start our journey up through a winding road of lush, pristine forest with great views of mountains, waterfalls, and Bhutan's abundant flora. Overnight at Hotel in Thimphu

Most haunting a call to prayer from a mosque in the vicinity, haunting and I find it deeply disturbing. In the pre-dawn hours sequestered in a dark room I feel exiled to the end of the world and more than ever in this trip *nostos* overtakes me. What are we doing in this place that is not India and does not feel like Bhutan? Is it that the gate to the land of Shangri-La passes through Purgatory?

....

At Hotel Pedling in the capital city of Bhutan Thimphu we wrap up the evening of a long day with brandy, the local stuff. It took nine hours on the road from Phuntsholing to Thimphu, hours filled with fine dust that chokes everything on the road including travelers inside their vehicles. A project started three years ago to widen the road is still in progress and nearly everything is hand made.

....

We finally leave the dusty, dark and run down Druk Hotel crammed inside a small but new bus the agency in Bhutan has put at our disposal. The luggage will travel separately in a taxi that is filled beyond capacity. Elaine and Lori sit in front and are able to raise their leg on some support. Marta as usual has her double seat in front by herself, while Cassandra gets the most forward single seat and no apologies. Our new guide Likhy from Bhutan is a pleasant young fellow with previous experience and fluent in English.

After going through the first immigration checkpoint we enter the work zone of the National Highway getting a taste of things to come. A queue of vehicles forms both ways while waiting for a portion of the road to be opened to traffic again. Heavy machinery is used in that portion to move tons of rock and earth. As the travel resumes we pass a segment of the road that has a collection of small steel sheet shacks put up in orderly rows at the side of the steep ravine.

- Temporary housing for imported labor from India and Bangladesh, the guide informs us.

The further we advance the more human misery we see, men, women and children working with hand tools to mix concrete, move large rocks, break stones, shovel, dig and sweat. They seem Bengali or Bangladeshi. You wonder what kind of life this is or how they survive. Food is delivered to them by trucks, food they have to pay for. All those guest workers are kept under close watch, welcomed temporarily until their usefulness is no more.

If you look towards India before the plains disappear behind steep mountain sides, you can see dense haze and multiple smoke plumes shrouding the region in brown screen. Ahead blue skies, clouds and clinging to the road dust puffballs. Look at the foliage the one not marred by the white powder, the deep chasm and the massive boulders, the Himalaya rising. But Bhutan, where is it? The Bhutan we thought of as unspoiled, naive and welcoming?

....

The main street of Thimphu at night is full of people wandering aimlessly or going someplace. A trade show, remainder of Bhutan's fifth king's coronation is lit up and so is the new luxury hotel. Many shops are now targeting the tourist, the rest are slowly shrinking and unavoidably closing down. The country is undergoing a profound transformation under the royal rule and the approval of India that moves freely its military throughout Bhutan. Perhaps we are making this trip too late...

Thimphu, Bhutan 16 November 2008

1.15

Day 9: Sightseeing in Thimphu Valley. (Nov 17) Sightseeing in the capital city will include a visit to the National Library, stocked with ancient Buddhist manuscripts, and a school where traditional art is kept alive through instruction in the art of painting Thangkhas (sacred Buddhist religious scrolls). We also visit a traditional medical institute where medicines are prepared according to ancient practices. We will also stop in at the Heritage Museum and Textile Museum. After lunch we visit Lungtenzampa to observe the royal traditional silversmiths at work, as well as see traditional Bhutanese paper making. We continue our sightseeing by visiting an incense factory, and the National Memorial Stupa and Drupthob Nunnery Temple.

Thimphu at 8,000 feet is colder than the plains. The sky is clear blue while the surrounding mountains mostly bare dark blue with brown patches imbedded. Monday of the third week traveling, the excitement has been replaced by a sensation of normal life, early rise, shower, breakfast, the bus, the company of others.

....

It is a packed day with tourist destinations around Thimphu. John Bird who is feeling better chooses to stay in bed leaving Gene in charge. It occurs to me he may feel the day's events are not worth the trouble.

The morning wind makes for biting cold. In the sun you can feel some warmth but for the time being everyone in the lobby is bundled. I enjoyed two Bhutanese flapjacks with local honey for breakfast and I am promised more for tomorrow morning. I smile at the thought. Gene says the bus has trouble starting. We are out in the sun and the morning wind, we wait.

Until a replacement bus arrives we go on foot to the National Handicrafts Center. The place was founded by the previous queen in support of the local handicrafts. Inside they are some beautiful samples of local handicrafts but we find the prices to border on the astronomical.

Eventually the replacement bus arrives to take us to the National Library where ancient Buddhist manuscripts are stored along with a woodblock press and random other books on Bhutan and Buddhism. One ascends to the top of the four Library floors by wooden stairs whose steps are capped with copper and in the usual Bhutanese habit have unequal heights. Before we leave we buy two copies of a prayer book printed on the woodblock press on handmade paper. The employee wraps each book carefully in red cloth.

The school where traditional handicrafts are taught is nearby. At the drawing class we get to meet Jimmy (Jigme) a talented young man who gives us a photocopy of a picture he has drawn, then we talk with another student in the wood carving class who is finishing details of a seven-string musical instrument. Not far from the school there is a retail store which we visit.

For lunch the Blue Lotus offers a Bhutanese fare, including the best up to now *ema datse*. Then the visits go on, to the Traditional Medical Institute, the National Memorial Stupa, the Drupthob Nunnery, Thimphu Dzong, paper making workshop and Tangkha painting shop. We are exhausted and not quite ready for another day on the road.

Thimphu, Bhutan 17 November 2008

* *1.16*

Day 10: Thimphu to Phobjikha. (Nov 18) Leaving Thimphu the road climbs steeply through a forest of pine and cedar, festooned with hanging lichen high up near the 10,000-foot Dochula pass and offering panoramic views of the Himalayan mountain ranges. We then descend through rhododendron, magnolia, juniper, and pine forests filled with the chirping of the many rare birds found in Bhutan. Upon arriving at Wangdue Phodrang, lunch will be served at Dragon Resort overlooking the calm Punatsangchu River. We then drive to Wangdue town and visit the majestic Dzong located on the spur of a hill at the confluence of the Tsang Chu and Dang Chu rivers. After strolling the one-street market of Wangdue we continue our drive to Phobjikha, with occasional stops for pictures, bird watching, and scenery. Once at Phobjikha we check into the Dewachen Hotel. If time permits, we can explore the valley on our own.

Ready to move out of Thimphu to the countryside where mobile phones and electricity work part-time, but rare species of birds overwinter. I don't find the capital of Bhutan particularly attractive, unlike most of the members of the group. Its natural setting is spare, the buildings uniform and its charm limited in spite of the river that runs through it. It is situated in a basin that could trap air pollutants if there is no wind blowing. We will see Thimphu once more returning from this two-day excursion.

Today the group is losing Cassandra and Marta who are flying out of Paro back to the States for reasons that concern Marta's job. No one seems to be sorry for the loss; they have behaved rather rudely to everyone all along.

....

The lights out with only a candle in the room in Phobjikha's Dewachen Hotel I sit to write at the table with the little wood stove purring softly and the boiling water pot hissing. Outside is cold, the mountain cold of high altitude that pierces one's bones.

....

Getting out of Thimphu on our way east to Phobjikha Valley we catch glimpses of the expanding town and the smoke trapped in the cold morning that engulfs parts of it. The foothills become more forested and greener. The first Dzhong of Thimphu perched on top of a hill dominates the entrance to the valley.

The bus keeps climbing higher on one of the best roads we experienced in this trip, one entirely surrounded by forests of mixture of tree types that, near the Dochula high pass, are replaced entirely by conifers. At the summit of the pass, 108 stupas are standing as a memorial to Bhutanese military killed in the clash with Nepali immigrants. The view from the summit of the stupa knoll is spectacular. 200 miles of snow-capped Himalayan peaks ring the horizon. In the morning transparent cerulean haze blends with the azure sky. Picture after picture, no photographer feels satisfied with having captured the awesome beauty of something beyond this earth.

The bus now begins to descend running through the reverse vegetation spectrum to that of the ascent. At the end of the descent the bus zigzags in parallel course with Punatsangchu River. We pass by apple orchards in fall foliage, the fruit already collected and ready for the market. An old town in the hills above is built with rammed earth and is in need of repairs. At the bend of the road next the bridge at the Immigration Control several vendors are selling fruit and fried rice crackers. The bus stops for paperwork, the passengers cross the bridge toward the town on the hill above where the oldest Bhutan Dzong looms.

We enter the Dzong which is still in use for administrative and religious activities. There is a Buddhist school on the premises with young students in recess. Many of the younger students not only do not mind but actually like having their photograph taken. The Dzong is impressive in spite of its condition but unlike most European forts and castles, only the courtyard can be visited.

Lunch is served at a nearby restaurant with well-prepared Bhutanese food adapted to foreign tastes. I find that I cannot retain memories of individual plates. Everything blends together like the little scoops on the buffet plates, leaving behind only a sense of overall pleasure.

After lunch the journey to Phobjikha resumes, slowly ascending to yet another 10,500 feet pass. The road is eroded and dusty; there are trees whose foliage is turning gold and red and many waterfalls that send water rushing over or under the road surface.

Here and there rhododendrons are scattered throughout and at the summit a view of the snowcapped peaks.

The Phobjikha Valley, winter home to the black-neck cranes, opens up, a wide expanse of high altitude dwarf bamboo, dotted with houses and farms although it is mostly an intact large flat bowl encircled by mountains. Somewhere down by the water streams the cranes are foraging.

The rustic hotel is a beautiful lodge in the Bhutanese style of architecture above the valley on the western slopes of the hills surrounded by farmhouses. We are informed that electricity is on from 17:30 to 21:00 and so is hot water. The rooms are equipped with small wood stoves that are already burning. Dinner is at 19:00 as usual. We put down the luggage and take a short walk before dark sets in.

Phobjikha, Bhutan 18 November 2008

1.17

Day 11: Phobjikha to Punakha. (Nov 19) After breakfast we explore the Phobjikha Valley, winter home for the rare black-necked crane which migrates from the central Asiatic Plateau to escape the harsh winters there. The valley itself is a realm of high altitude dwarf bamboo, the favorite food of yaks. We will visit the Gangtey Monastery perched atop a small hill that rises from the valley floor. The monastery is surrounded by a large village inhabited mainly by the families of the 140 gomchens who take care of the monastery. The only Nyingmapa monastery in western Bhutan and the largest in the country, it is headed by its spiritual master, the ninth Gangtey Tulku.

Rest and a good shower at Meri-Phunsum Resort are refreshing and restful following another day of long drive and two hikes.

....

I wake up before the cranes and all other birds; the alarm clock has gone off. I watch the faint predawn light sensing the morning cold. I know the wood stove is cold, hot water is tepid and there is no electricity. Elaine encourages me to stay in bed longer which I do, ten more minutes until dawn proper enters. Somehow I manage to shave with a flashlight and a candle. I open the drapes to see the frozen world of Phobjikha; a bird flies by, a crow. The valley shrouded in mist and clouds of smoke is stirring from its slumber. The view is enchanting.

After breakfast I join a party from the group that intends to hike to the Gangtey Goemba on a small hill a couple of miles from the hotel. We start together but soon we split as different people pursue their photographic interests and elusive black-necked cranes views. After one half hour of hiking, the bus with the remaining group stops to pick us up for the visit of the monastery. The monastery is surrounded by a village of *gomchens* (caretakers) and their families. It is now undergoing restoration and partial rebuilding by private funding. The place is as large as a Dzong but the big courtyard and surrounding buildings evoke New World Missions.

The way to Punaka uses the same road we took to get here. Near the destination we stop at the restaurant Dragon's Nest overlooking the Punatsangchu River. Another well prepared mostly vegetarian lunch awaits us and most of all a clean bathroom.

After lunch a short hike takes us Chimi Lhakhang Temple dedicated to Drukpa Kuenley known as Divine Madman. The path runs through rice fields that have recently been harvested. The small temple is atop a small hill. While walking there we have some fine views of the river and the terraced rice fields. The temple itself fails to attract me even though it is a popular pilgrimage for many.

The place for our night stay is modern and well-kept surrounded by gardens on a steep hill. As with the rest of the hotels in this trip there are problems with plumbing and electricity. Still we need and have a nice shower and some quiet time to ourselves.

Punaka, Bhutan 19 November 2008

1.18

Day 12: Punaka to Thimpu. (Nov 20) After breakfast we will proceed to Punakha town to view the majestic Dzong (fortress), situated between the two rivers Pho Chu and Mochu (male and Female River). This fortress is now used as the winter seat of the Je Khenpo (the Spiritual head of Bhutan). In the past this Dzong served as the capital seat of the country for 300 years. After the visit of the Dzong we will resume our journey to Thimphu, en route we will take a short 40 minutes' walk to Chimi Lhakhang Temple situated on a small hill. This temple is dedicated to the great Yogi in 14th century known as Drukpa Kuenley or popularly known as "Divine madman" to the westerners. It is believed that this temple blesses women who seek fertility. We will continue our drive uphill after a good lunch at YT hotel crossing the Dochula Pass, if due to bad weather we missed the panoramic view of Bhutan's 200 miles of majestic snowcapped peaks that border Tibet earlier this might be your best chance. Overnight at hotel in Thimphu. In the evening you are invited for a dinner at Private house where you will be joined by Bhutanese Dignitaries and some folk dances.

Bhutan confuses me, I cannot place it in my personal geography correctly, one time it is China, another South East Asia and sometimes when I look at children's faces, South America. Its inhabitants' persona is curious but its geographic identity is confusing with tropical, moderate and alpine zones all put together as a continuum over steep mountainsides. I think I have come to like it better after a few days here though I still have trouble relating to a culture that is abruptly being transformed after centuries of Buddhist theocracy.

....

After a leisurely breakfast the bus drives to the imposing Punaka Dzong. The Dzong built in the 17th century is situated at the confluence of river Pho Chhu and Mo Chhu and connects to the other bank with an impressive bridge that was rebuilt recently. The fort is also reconstructed and serves as winter seat of Bhutan's spiritual head. The town that surrounded the fort has been demolished after a catastrophic flood in the 60s when 20 people perished and it has been replaced by a new settlement further up on higher ground.

Jigme provides a brief history of the construction of the Dzong, more than half of which is folk myth as is most of Bhutan's history until the 20th Century. We stand by the joining of the rivers in the park of the Superior High School across the road. Schoolgirls, undisturbed, study for their exams, kingfishers and cormorants dive in the waters in search of a meal. The cool breeze sends shivers down the spine while sun and clouds do battle for the mastery of the day.

You don't realize the true size of the Dzong until you cross the bridge that has been magnificently fashioned by modern Bhutanese craftsmen. Inside there are three courtyards, majestic buildings decorated with Buddhist stories and symbols in lively colors and gold leaf. Last we enter a magnificent temple where the new king has been crowned on November 2 this year. Beautifully and richly decorated it is almost the jewel of the crown. Likhy narrates the story of Siddhartha Gautama Buddha painted in several wall-sized murals and explains many unfamiliar objects and their significance. By the time we exit the temple everyone shivers from the cold of the temple inside, something we have experienced in most temples and monasteries. Slowly we take our earthly bodies out of this otherworldly experience whose architectural design was handed over to the chosen architect in his dream as myth relates the story. The sun is shining and burns the skin as if trying to rid your material self.

The road goes up and up, grudgingly the bus climbs slowly towards Dochula Pass. When the Himalayan peaks become visible again clouds protect them from profaning eyes or cameras. Near the summit a halt for lunch takes us to YT Hotel where we get to taste butter tea for the first time. Particularly good are the mustard greens, while the beef which I chose, thinking it was mushrooms, I think of as Yak meat for its toughness.

Back in Thimphu at Hotel Pedlin we are now on the top floor. We take a walk in the main street of the city. Since no physician visit could be arranged for Elaine we need to get some medical supplies. We also visit the Swiss Bakery by the hotel for a birthday dessert treat, and then we turn in to prepare for this evening's invitation to dinner at the house of the owner of the travel agency Sierra Club uses in Bhutan.

We are greeted by our hosts Benchen Khenpo Rinpoche, his wife Tashi Wangmo, and Tanga the marketing manager of Benchen's business. In the living room we meet Datsi, a young Bhutanese who has lived for years in Los Angeles and related to the family. She is there with her husband Robert, a Canadian who now works for the Bank of Bhutan. The son of Benchen and Tashi is a 9-year old lively and mischievous boy who meddles in everything.

Drinks, including *arra*, are poured while we wait for the Bhutanese dignitaries to arrive. A list is placed on the table that reads:

LIST OF DIGNITARIES INVITED TONIGHT
MINISTRY OF HOME & CULTURAL AFFAIRS
    Honorable Minister Lyonpo Minjur Dorji
    General V. Namgyal, ADC (Aide-de- camp) to His Majesty the 4th King
    Honorable Former Minister Lyonpo Leki Dorji
    Honorable Secretary, Dasho Sherub Tenzin, Cabinet Secretariat.
    Honorable Secretary, Dasho Tashi Phuntshog, Advisor Legal & Cultural Affairs
    Honorable Judge, Dasho Jigme Zangpo, High Court.
    Dasho Kezang Wangdi, Director General, Tourism Council of Bhutan

Soon enough the dignitaries arrive along with a folkloric dance group. We end up talking to the Minister of Home and Culture whose origins are in the East Bhutan.

Before dinner we are treated to an unexpected birthday celebration with beautiful scarves and cakes that Benchen himself offers to Elaine and me. Afterwards we move to a dining area for a sampling of well-prepared dishes, more conversation and folkloric dancing.

Around 22:00, late by Bhutanese standards, we thank our hosts and walk out to return to the hotel for tomorrow's trip. Likhy remains behind and seems a bit tipsy.

Thimphu, Bhutan 20 November 2008

* *1.19*

Day 13: Thimpu- Paro. (Nov 21) After breakfast we will visit Thimphu weekend market, which is in a permanent set of stalls, vendors from throughout the region arrive on Friday afternoon and remain selling their goods until Sunday night. It's an interesting place to visit, where village people jostle with well-heeled Thimphu residents for the best - and cheapest – vegetables and foodstuffs. This is the only time that fresh produce is easily available and the shopping is enhanced by the opportunity to catch up on the week's gossip. At the northern end of the market is a collection of stalls called the indigenous goods and handicrafts section. Here you will find locally produced goods, including religious objects, baskets, fabrics and different hats from various minority groups. We will then start our drive to Paro, this will take about two hours. In Paro we will visit Drukgyal Dzong built in 1647 by Shubdrung Nawang Namgyal, the Dzong was destroyed by fire and left in ruins as an evocative reminder of the great victories it was built to commemorate. On a clear day you can get a magnificent view of the Mount Chomolhari, alt. 7314 m / 23,990 ft. Drive south to Satsam Chorten, built in memory of the late Dilgo Khentse Rinpochey, and continue on to Kyichu Lhakhang, built in seventh century by a Tibetan King, Songtsen Gonpo and walk through the one street Paro town. After lunch visit the National Museum of Bhutan, (Ta Dzong) which contains works of art, handicrafts, costumes, armor and rare stamps. Take a leisurely hike down to Rimpung Dzong. You will walk through a traditional covered bridge across the river to one street Paro market, after an hour of strolling around the market you will then driven to your hotel.

Two glasses of *arra* did not give me a hangover though two glasses of red wine had some effect on Elaine. Thinking of Bhutan I feel sad to see that the country is at the edge of a precipice. The change is coming from within and without; danger lurks in the adoption of Western ways the communications media have introduced and the pressure of its powerful neighbors. The best hope is the development of strong eco-friendly tourism to help maintain high living standards.

....

It seems like a very long day then we finally arrive to the last hotel outside of Paro that is run-down and not too clean. Elaine's bruise looks horrible, continues to ooze serum and does not allow her to participate in the more vigorous activities of the trip. It makes me apprehensive; I wish we could instantly transport home.

....

Out of Thimphu the bus retraces steps of the arrival until we reach the crossroads to Paro Valley by an Immigration Control point. The bus stops, the passengers cross the bridge to the other side. On the bridge a Bhutanese family drags a dead dog and throws the body over the parapet to the rushing clear waters of Paro River.

We board the bus again to Paro following the course of the river. There is a certain similarity to an Argentine *quebrada* though the valley narrows as we advance. The landscape is parched with little vegetation. Further north we see many rice and potato fields at the wide riverbed.

The National Museum housed in Ta Dzong is labyrinthine with treacherous steps and in places very low ceilings. It contains an eclectic collection of Bhutanese historical items of all sorts. At the exit I opt to walk with some of the group to Rimpung Dzong. The hike is steep and dusty, the cold wind rages over an unattractive landscape. This Dzong cannot be compared to the splendid Punaka Dzong. Access to the interior is through a series of stone stairs whose uneven steps make climbing difficult.

The program includes a visit to the remains of the Drukgyal Dzong at a high point with vistas of the Chomolari peak and to the seventh century Kyichu Lhakhang. The light of the day slowly wanes; I feel tired.

Paro, Bhutan 21 November 2008

1.20

Day 14: Excursion to the Tiger's Nest. (Nov 22) Hike to Taktshang Monastery, the most famous of Bhutan's monasteries. Taktshang means "Tiger's Nest," so named because Guru Rimpoche reportedly flew to the site of the monastery on the back of a flying tiger in the early centuries of the first millennium. The monastery is perched on a cliff nearly 3,000 ft above the Paro valley floor. This day hike is not only historically and culturally interesting, but also incredibly scenic!

They are my company one cat, one dog and two playful puppies. The puppies have found the pieces of cookie and eat it. The cat had the piece I gave it and lies in abandon on top of the trestle, soaking sun. The mother dog is being pursued by her puppies. A spotted nutcracker flies from treetop to treetop calling and in the background the sound of rushing water. Two French tourists pass in search of a restroom, two Russian tourist huff and puff uphill to visit Tiger's Nest. That is life around Taktshang Tea House where I sit waiting for the rest of the group to show up for lunch.

....

Is it morning or the moon? I lie awake waiting for the sound of the alarm clock. The time is 04:35, the cold getting more intense though there is no sound of wind. In the morning hike to Taktshang Monastery who will be there, will the hike be too strenuous, etc. etc. I wish we were already home though we will try to make the best of today. Tomorrow morning early we will be up packing for the arduously long trip back.

....

We board the bus in the morning cold. The bus drives away towards the beginning of the trail where horses will await for four of the party while the rest climb on foot. Other tourist buses are on their way, we'll have company! Another world-site is overrun by crowds.

The climb is steep, the breathing hard and the sun bright and warm enough to make us shed the outer layer. Sally huffs and puffs with determination taking one step after another; she will make it. Apparently a marathon runner in her forties she has been athletic most of her life. Slowly we climb higher, the forest composition changes, there are evergreen oaks scattered among the pines and some rhododendrons. Old trees are covered with hanging moss and occasionally studded with fern colonies. We reach the point where the trail divides going to the Dzong or to the Tea House. There by the stupa the horses munch on green foliage. The riders mount again to continue to the point where the steps begin. We follow on foot encountering others going up, making short stops to allow our breath to catch up with the climbing pace. There are stupas and a sign in Bhutanese, water runs down in little streams. At the second vista our companions wait. This is where we part; I descend to the Tea House, preferring to avoid the steep and uneven Bhutanese steps.

.....

The wind kicks up; from the trail the forms of our companions are dark shadows in the dust storm. We all move inside the Tea House for lunch and take seats in the round. The food is vegetarian Indian except for *ema datse* and very good.

....
We descend quickly, John Bird and I, to find the bus waiting for the group. The driver, Norbu has been with the people left behind, shuttling them between the hotel and the town of Paro. Now he is here for us, courteous and smiling. This is probably his last tour for the year. The rest of the time until the tourist season will open in late September, he will be at home in Paro with his family farming and doing whatever is necessary for survival.

....
Our last stop is at Paro for last minute gift purchases. Paro's shopping district is diminutive and consists of many small shops usually with poor selections. I go along with David, Desiree and Gene to pass the time because my heart is not in shopping. The cold wind blows in the streets and empty lots of the town, the cold clear light of the setting sun is oblique, the shadows dark and inhospitable. Three-story buildings block the view of hills and mountains. In a weaving shop I stand near the space heater that warms a quartet of young women weavers. I am ready to bid Bhutan goodbye.

Paro, Bhutan 22 November 2008

1.21
Day 15: Depart Paro- Bangkok/ Delhi (Nov 23) Transfer to airport for your onward flight to Bangkok or Delhi.

A huge airport to deal with, thankfully we have reserved a room at NOVOTEL in the airport. We get shuttled there. We try to balance our physical and emotional state. Elaine has her wound dressed by the hotel nurse, the resident "doctor".

I feel exhausted after yesterday's hike, bad sleep and early morning waking. We look forward to being home. Still we are many hours away.

Bangkok International Airport
November 23 2008

Approaching the West Coast of North America in the plane, a shell filled with passengers, I feel relieved to see this trip come to an end. Its downturns have overshadowed the pleasures of discovering a different world. Thus having crossed the International Dateline I have turned my clock back to a familiar metronome that guides our lives.

Flight CX782 November 24 2008

* *1.22*

Long period of illness keeps me silent, each day hopeful for improvement that is slow to come; I suffer this period oppressed and glum traveling dark paths of the mind. The nights come too soon though dawns are a world away, little can be accomplished, smiles are not part of winter landscape without bright sun. Elaine's soul has descended in a vortex of obsession with the ugly wound as I regret the trip to India-Bhutan, as both counterproductive exercises.

Fiddletown 12 December 2008

* *1.23*

The year comes to an end; I feel neither regretful nor pleased with its impending demise, I think of it as unimportant as repeating events are, the leaves that drop in autumn, and the wind that rushes through the valley or the cool of the morning. Then the year is gone in an auto-da-fe that is meaningless.

Fiddletown 29 December 2008

1.24

Long irrigation lines extended on the width of the walnut orchard, wrapped in new grass or buried in soft soil before I neatly coiled them to lie against steel stakes. It is now winter calling for trees to be pruned, fertilized and made ready during their deep sleep.

Not today or tomorrow, those are days we celebrate the New Year with long-distance calls to friends and abundant food and wine. Not today or tomorrow, as I open up the cupboards of memory to let shadows flit out.

Next year I promise to take the horse by the bridle and the pruning pole out in the wintry light of day.

   Fiddletown 31 December 2008

1.25

St John the Baptist Day of Epiphany I recall celebrated in my school days with the throwing of the Cross in the waters of Peneus River to be retrieved by the young men who defied the winter cold for a blessing and a photo in the local newspapers. Today as the day of celebration for friends living in Greece compels me to call them and temporarily re-connect.

Newspapers will undergo a profound transformation in this digitally connected world. I fear that old journalistic icons will be here no more within a decade, if that. I confess to being a less than regular newspaper reader and have always been so. I marveled at people who spent hours reading those awkwardly large pages, in timeworn Greek cafes with a thimbleful of thick coffee and a glass of water. Another world going away as if lost in the vanishing pages of the publication itself...

   Fiddletown 6 January 2009

* *1.26*

Years pass, lives perish, still the wheel of perception inexorably repeats the manifestations of impermanence with a regularity we term time. Everything is different yet the same to signal we have made no significant progress, just circular paths without marks.

I count twenty years since the passing of a good friend by his own hand, I count thirty years since meeting another good friend and the carrying out of a landmark journey.

   Fiddletown 7 January 2009

* *1.27*

Yesterday a different world on the outside of our speed-driven humanity almost remote and unconnected a handsome rooster crossing the street unconcerned the cars come to a stop quiet the immersion in the waters of season entirely out of synch with human calendar one stands by the park with a small amphitheater reverting to past memories when where and all that not far from a river of water and rivers of automobiles in the streets of Fair Oaks

  ....

The last effort it seemed as another chance at reversing youthful failure her face in mists hidden to reach an agreement impossible or non-negotiable whichever only fetters and seals fate as it has been the clear voice murmurs in dreams only what I had desired passing up offers because the possible is worthless the dance of hours the echo of miscalculations the flowers in midwinter mock history's side streets

  ....

Gradually we return to the rhythm we deviated from because of the November trip and its aftermath. If only mending the economy would be as easy and straightforward. The new President has a formidable task ahead; I wish him well and I want to believe he has the interests of the country and of humanity at heart. Time will show. Meanwhile I need to get the farm fully cleaned and prepared for springtime. The rain has yet to come, I don't despair reasoning the storm gate is about to open.

Fiddletown 14 January 2009

1.28

Clouds spread across the horizon signal the end of good weather. Pruning began; the first trees already shorn of unnecessary brush look vulnerable in the cold morning light. I rub the back of my neck, stiff from looking up while pruning high branches, reflecting on yesterday's inauguration, which saddens me strangely because I see in it the fleeting aspect of human affairs, feeling sorry even for George W. Bush who seems resigned to his future unimportance. A new guard has moved in, faces to become familiar and names to be repeated a thousand times, all the others of the departing order already rattle in the dustbin. Barak Obama, strange name for an American President, has reached for his dream and seized it almost effortlessly. To be in the right place at the right time is part of the formula. Now the weight of the country and of the world has been placed on his shoulders...

Fiddletown 21 January 2009

1.29

Balmy days do not bring much rain compounding fears of severe drought after three years of dry conditions. The economy is in severe drought as well, reminding me of Pharaoh's dream of the ten fat and ten thin cows, only we were not prudently advised to save for the impoverished years ahead. Then we reap what we sow, which is illusion.

It took a number of days to rebuild the Moto Q back to its former level after I decided to upgrade it to Windows Mobile

6.1 version. I had forgotten how much work went in customizing it with applications and modifications supporting the display of Chinese Unicode characters. Now at its previous level, it will remain stable for a longer period.

> Fiddletown 2 February 2009

* *1.30*

Tasked to pass through life as a sprite that leaves no memory only a vivid impression extinguished so soon after, thus we are all forms of complex life on our part of cosmos. Memories can only exist in us, in other similar systems obeying to similar principles and also highly evolved, memories are fabrications evoking events that even in their most accurate description could not be faithful to the original. Of course they are codifications that make any sense at all only to the system that has the required keys; to others they remain meaningless as history vanishes swiftly.

> Fiddletown 9 February 2009

* *1.31*

White, white outside falling in small pieces from a white sky and covering everything under uniform coat, then the landscape loses its colors as if touched by a transforming spell. I did not expect snow, I did not expect the electricity to fail but it does in a most startling fashion. Now we have to rearrange the day, to light the woodstove, read or write and stay inside again. The landscape that looks so beautiful to unaccustomed eyes I grow easily tired of; no I would not thrive in harsh winter land, already I miss the sun gone for a few hours.

> Fiddletown 13 February 2009

1.32

Shivers, shooting pain, sensitive areas of the skin developing a rash, I know them since yesterday as symptoms of shingles. In heavy rain to the Medical Offices in Rancho Cordova, seeking the cause for the neck and shoulder worsening pain; I never seriously considered this unpleasant option.

The drop dead date for the TV HD conversion has come and gone though it has been optionally reset to June 12. I would rather have seen them hold on steadfast to the original deadline. The true problems that underlie the new technology will show after analog broadcasting is completely turned off.

Fiddletown 18 February 2009

1.33

The shingles rash at its peak makes the right side of my neck unsightly, red and bumpy like a heinous disease that befell in ancient times, mark of a wrathful and unforgiving God. After a painful night during which I had to force myself to sleep, a sheer delight to walk about relishing hints of springtime before the next storm arrives.

Fiddletown 21 February 2009

1.34

KP Folsom Medical Center one half hour to noon. Outside it is raining, a steady cold rain the wind shifts and molds to sheets or showers. The place is full of people waiting, arriving or leaving. Elaine is here for an ultrasound scan then we will follow the medical trail to Rancho Cordova for a shingles vaccine and another prescription of analgesic pills for me. I suffer still with pain radiating from the right side of the head and neck area even as the rash has dried out gradually effacing itself from that area. The skin is rough and too painful to touch, even my tongue when receiving the first morsel of food or drink sends an electric like shock cascading in the palate. I suffer silently waiting for any signs of amelioration which seem to arrive painfully slowly.

    Fiddletown 3 March 2009

* *1.35*

Horrid news: cancer without a remission chance for Karen Mickel. On the telephone the voice of her husband sounds broken. How can one ever express his or her own true feelings of regret and sympathy?

    Elaine doesn't want to think about the irreversibility that death introduces to our lives.

    Fiddletown 11 March 2009

* *1.36*

Slowly the feeling of health returns starting with sleep and normal dreams interrupted only on occasion with flashes of pain or uncontrolled itching that prickling can cause. The night before I was in a commutator state processing a long queue of inbound messages, one slight tickle, an urge to shift the body to different position, a jab of pain along the back of the neck, an indeterminate sound and many other not so decipherable messages. Meanwhile Fritz and Linda slept deeply after a long train ride in the next room. Fritz is the only link I have from my days at Caltech. We see each other every few years while time keeps moving fast.

    Fiddletown 18 March 2009

* *1.37*

    A quiet voice speaks...

Της θάλασσας τα κύματα της νύχτας τα πελάγη της κοπελιάς τα χείλη έσβησαν τι μόνο αδράχτι χάνεται στα φύλλα φθινοπώρου
A voice long silent stirs in the nocturnal space spanning dreams seeking its long lost domain...

    Fiddletown 2 April 2009

* *1.38*

Seeing any of Visconti's late masterpieces is a visual treat which educates the eye in the art of light, color and design appreciation. *Ludwig* belongs to this category with opulent use of color and chiaroscuro.

This morning when I open the blinds I gaze upon the ridge to the east that is swathed in fog and a brilliant sun, just clearing the horizon while framed by dark clouds, extends its rays through soft brume gauze. All this lasts a few seconds before the landscape is plunged in the gray muted colors of winter. Only the white bloom of certain trees stands out cheerfully to remind us of the spring.

    Fiddletown 11 April 2009

* *1.39*

Sunlight filters in the room; abruptly a long restless night comes to end. Here at The Donatello again after twenty two years about to celebrate the forty fourth anniversary, how have things changed? In the mirror someone else unrecognizable watches every move with piercing suspicious eyes, someone you ought to remember but you refuse to. The weather in San Francisco will be milder today, no chance of rain and maybe even the wind will be still.

Kent and his wife from Cincinnati at the next table finish their dinner happy to be on vacation in California. At Plouf where mussels are consumed by the bucket in search of *moules marin-*

ières and *frites* a mild disappointment. Nevertheless we overeat and each step of the return to the hotel seems overly laborious.

....
Sarah Choy is congenial; I spent most of the time at Café Grillade talking to her while Phil Choy describes ambiguities of Chinese language to Elaine. How is it possible to understand the true meaning of such language without a complete frame of reference?

....
Wind blows fiercely all day. At Golden Gate Park crowds gather to frolic or gawk at exhibits, ultimately everyone being one. A Museum building defies Nature that surrounds it with a manifesto proclaiming it fits in the landscape, behemoth with copper hide and an upside observation tower. An enclosed garden claims Shakespeare and one with winding path exacts tolls to trespassers.

....
The Muni line that joins Union Square with this part of town masquerades as a rail trolley that leisurely winds through the neighborhood streets once it leaves underground passages in which it accelerated to Metro-Line speeds.

....
Pad Kee Mao at the Thai Noodle Café and Tom Yum noodle soup after delicious Thai *somosas*, reward for a morning of museum loitering. The Muni line threads through the center of the street and an old grizzled person in army camouflage fatigue and hat sells the STREET GAZETTE.

....
Our anniversary celebration at Kuleto's with John and Lori keeps us out of the blustery weather until we return to the hotel.

S. F. 25 April 2009

1.40

A better night despite the wee hours of the morning noisy neighbors provides a much needed rest. I did not dream I think until little memory fragments begin to coalesce. Late breakfast at Zuni Café, Bhutan reunion of sorts precedes the visit to the Asian Art Museum with John, Lori, David and Desirée.

   S. F. 26 April 2009

1.41

Illness everywhere floats like weeds on the surface of the pond of our life and of others, obscuring the shape of things and marring beauty. Bob Allen is seriously ill at home now after a brain surgery for which I was given little information. Following a herpes zoster attack with strength sapped he remains at home. Karen is slowly and painfully dying while her husband hopelessly helps in all meaningful ways he can. Swine flu, newsmongers and governments tell us, nearly a pandemic that threatens humanity with becoming one of the scourges to be inflicted by Nature. In the morning sunlight I try to evoke beauty from years past.

   Fiddletown 29 April 2009

1.42

Rain intermittent comes in squalls leaving behind window panes smeared with water fluid images dissolve and reconstitute themselves fantastic shapes and green shadows murmuring the same story innumerable times the winter that has passed the land will visit it again and again

   Fiddletown 3 May 2009

*1.43

Smooth forehead with nearly invisible bumps somewhere in the left half yet a large dark spot as smooth as the surrounding area as you ponder about people that have whom we know of from written testimony informal or formal history documents life-like wind that carried seeds far away within a larger existential sphere than any of us will explore suffice to say it is impossible to contain all recollections given to a being during a lifetime the individual a large pomegranate bursting out full of ruby seeds

   Fiddletown 15 May 2009

*1.44

Night dappled intricate and colorful designs of the Persian rug remain silent not speaking thoughts that wove them at dawn worlds collide and words cease to have a meaning in the beauty of a world dying to be reborn inside itself without reason like summer carelessly throwing open the windows to morning hope adorned with dew diamonds in the first sunlight thus I begin and end without limit repeating regrets and dimness of time before

   Fiddletown 22 May 2009

*1.45

Summer heat flows in from open windows, the bright sunlight reaches for the innermost corners of the house probing indifferently where dust has settled or desiccated insects lie waiting to turn to dust too. The open windows are quickly closed to hold a bit of morning freshness inside and the plans for the day are made.
 Susi and Isabelle depart for their Romania and Bavaria trip tomorrow and we have yet to wish them bon voyage.

Fiddletown 28 May 2009

* 1.46

Again and again reminders that an experience is fleeting unrepeatable tarnished with the sand of time and nothing is as powerful a reminder as the departure of a person close to you. So sudden has been Judy's passing that seemed unreal and numbing leaving us with memories and an indissoluble wall. What about Bernard?

Fiddletown 31 May 2009

* 1.47

June has brought gloom to N. California. Fog drapes vineyard hillsides and the green shades of new foliage grow darker. The thought of travel to the Northwest still remains only a thought because of other concerns or priorities whilst little by little its appeal diminishes. At times the economic downturn seems to bring more ills than just financial woes, shadow shifting the color and clarity of landscape.

Fiddletown 10 June 2009

* 1.48

Preparation for short vacation, all the same one has to go through the litany of checks, packing, provisioning for the cat, checking the timed drip-irrigation and finally work up all the anxiety in the world. I still think of my dream vacation, without preparations or packing, freely spontaneous...

Fiddletown 16 June 2009

1.49

Nights in strange places long confusing lost in memories like drifting sailboats those that age has gilded with its own ashes not suspecting traps other than the floating torn pieces of a long letter

....
Ashland remains still untouched by change, at least the part we see, its downtown area. As with places one has not lived in for an extended period of time, we must relearn quickly. To my surprise the layout of the city is different than I recalled. Finally we locate the motel we stayed during the last visit and take residence in it. The dark and musty room needs to have its silence aired. Raindrops hit the windows, a passing cloud that moves on.

A sort walk by the Shakespeare Festival Theater brings us to the upstairs of Martino's restaurant where patrons finish dinner before rushing to a performance. In the courtyard we sit under trees, umbrellas and an unsettled sky while having dinner. The morrow brings another long drive to Portland.

Ashland, OR 17 June 2009

1.50

A small luminous sliver over the western horizon slices the brooding darkness of clouds and the city this hour of nocturnal change bathes itself in electric light. There is something to Portland that can please most everyone emanating from its unpretentiousness and manageable size of its core settlement. Yet it is incapable of stirring any deep emotions in me, pleasantly inconsequential.

As the days pass my patience grows thinner. There is little I feel we have gained from this trip; the landscape is unimpressive and eroded from urban sprawl. Incensed by winery pretentions and prices, I consider those as symptoms that will lead to the downfall of the wine industry and retrenchment to the old value and position of wine. In the days of global economics such an event will impact all wine-producing countries. Will that be the next bubble to burst?

Mediocre food or good food in mediocre size or oversized bad food, all lead to the same conclusion, food is a serious matter and a matter of heart. The best food is home cooked, the worse is mass-prepared or pretense-executed, both bad for the heart!

       Portland, OR 19 June 2009

* *1.51*

From the window pearl gray light fills the room, quiet in a Saturday morning. The downtown of Portland feels uninhabited. In the beginning of each travel day I agonize to come up with a plausible and interesting schedule; why does one need to feel this way, why purpose becomes an unrelenting force? Anxiety rises from the depths of an unstructured time that needs justification.

Of Leonidas we thought because of the homonymous chocolate store yesterday morning. We hope he heals fully from his operation soon. We still think of him as he was in his visit in 2000 at the age of 8. The chocolates in the gold box on top of the desk have become both temptation and decoration. Leonidas thousands of miles from here is a thread in the wind of life.

       Portland, OR 20 June 2009

* *1.52*

Toward the western hills sun shines and where clouds let their shadow fall green turns to black adding a three-dimensional quality to the landscape. There will be sun today over Portland even if it shares the sky with brooding clouds. For the next couple of days a warming up to summer level temperatures is forecast with short cooling off to follow. This summer has entered on a mild note.

Yesterday we bought a baseball cap at the gift store of the Portland Chinese Garden. The Chinese characters stitched on the cap are supposed to say *gardener* but only one of them is identifiable as garden. The foibles of Chinese language are a linguistic Great Wall that makes learning the language exasperating. For the time being we must accept the meaning at inscrutable face value.

We will spend our last day in Portland visiting museums. Sunday should be a very quiet day in downtown Portland, a city whose center is not filled with life even on weekdays.

Portland, OR 21 June 2009

* *1.53*

The trip to Oregon is coming to an end tomorrow as we return home on Wednesday. The motel we chose to stay this time is not comfortable, it has little privacy and even less parking. It is a group of tiny cottages surrounded by a beautiful garden, all in need of some serious upgrades. For the time being we will stay here and try to ignore its shortcomings.

Summer finally has shown its face to S. Oregon with bright cerulean skies swept by cool breezes. Tomorrow even warmer temperatures are expected.

Ashland, OR 22 June 2009

* *1.54*

Remainders on the WWW like bread crumbs tracing a journey without purpose when I look up my own name nothing new old marks still persist for a while before the tide of time quietly will erase them

S. Oregon is like California, Mediterranean light and warmth, the sky with nary a cloud. The place we stay is still shrouded in tranquility, an orange cat crosses the path of my gaze soundlessly and a few cars roll out to the street, who knows wither. This, the last day of this vacation, everything we have done and travelled begins to acquire an extraordinary glow. Tomorrow and the days after tomorrow, the photographs processed and sorted, we may linger over them nostalgically knowing their experiences cannot be repeated ever.

  Ashland 23 June 2009

* *1.55*

The circle becomes smaller with each revolution, closer to the sun the wings begin to melt and the flesh is seared, forever turns to never and the eyes see their own shadow.

 In the morning it is time to pack and return where objects know your presence where work is part of daily schedule. Trees, vines and plants in the midday sun take the heat stoically, summer is already here.

  Fiddletown 24 June 2009

* *1.56*

At month's end the fiery hand of sun has seized the land as it besieges life with thirst.

  Fiddletown 29 June 2009

* *1.57*

Photographs, static representations of point in time reveal only the extensions of a living observer whose roving eye independent of time itself attaches significance to random events for aesthetic or historical motivations. The continuous motion broken to discrete steps opens multiple paths to parts of the time-space continuum and the spoken or written word breaks down.

Fiddletown 9 July 2009

1.58

The house is full of lavender perfume; July is the month for harvesting summer capsules from herb beds and filling space with blue and violet color to last through the winter. Absent-mindedly I take photographs of the world surrounding us to study them carefully later.

In the other room the awkward handwriting looks out from the side of an old trunk seeing such things I am no longer capable of. In memory, events and past experiences often take the dimension of improbable. I study each letter of the handwritten address carefully as if I were to discover a hidden message under the dusty coat of time...

Fiddletown 13 July 2009

1.59

Water flowing inside long black tubes at the time the program has been instructed to irrigate long lines going through sparse weeds that grow desperately as if trying to catch the thoughts of the spinning sun just intent to live forever

Fiddletown 16 July 2009

1.60

So quickly we arrived at the end of July, soon in August and the summer once more has left us with yearning for youth and carefree days which we wasted without purpose. Now again one has little purpose and even less future except for salvaging pieces of scattered lives to put together a mosaic in spite of all odds.

Here being in Petaluma it feels no different than any other town USA perhaps any other town in the world. Working day starts early, traffic never ceases, all services and products are standardized and prices keep rising. A couple of days away we agreed on, is this we bargained for?

    Petaluma 30 July 2009

* *1.61*

On Fridays there is an air of anticipation at the breakfast table, habit of working years that we cultivate still. The fruit bowl now is filled with orchard fruit of all colors and tempting savors. We talk of friends or daily worries, mundane topics and at times turn to philosophical subjects that lengthen our breakfast disproportionately. Next week, already on the horizon, begins to intrude in my thoughts...

    Fiddletown 8 August 2009

* *1.62*

Noise of engines, work in progress in the pond next door where dredging and widening is under way. RIP Chester Lake, you lived longer than your homonymous spiritual father. Solon wise of the human condition would not have been surprised, though I mourn his passing and the gradual destruction of the place whose Chester and Mary were its stewards for part of their lives...

    Fiddletown 19 August 2009

* *1.63*

Days become shorter as the *Decline of Fruit* sets in. September is poised to enter the gates of revolving time, those lying beyond the eastern ridge of the mountains. Man arrives, man departs but we are only aware of the departures of those who have been traveling with us for some time. Eulogy is humanity's measure.

    Fiddletown 30 August 2009

* *1.64*

Fruit hangs down to red earth lack of rain transforms to dust lumps of soil gradually reduced to small pieces scattered about under green foliage or blue sky whither now wind carry you the falling stars

    Fiddletown 1 September 2009

* *1.65*

If memory were as weak as light at great distances we would hardly recall the misfortunes that beset us; instead eight years past the moments of grand horror they are as vivid as now in the minds of the country. Later generational shifts will erase detail as it happens with the flow of time. Many lives lost and still we fail to be taught history's lessons.

    Fiddletown 11 September 2009

* *1.66*

Time's dimensionality is demonstrated plainly with time stamping each of the excerpts entered here. To my surprise something is captured in September, a very busy month in the farm.

    Fall makes its entrance with clouds, wind and chill; trees are shedding leaves overnight turned pale or gold. Fruit hangs heavy pulling down branches, birds scatter swooping through thin foliage. The house inside is darker without sunlight.

Fiddletown 29 September 2009

* *1.67*

The level of noise coming from a couple of tables next to me that host a group of women is insufferable. Caffeine Cuisine is now Shingle Springs Coffee Company. It is again filled with people; is the worst of the recession over?

Temperatures dropping dramatically make October feel wintrier than one would expect. Trees rush to shed their foliage showering traffic with multi-colored confetti. Autumn luminous has settled in the foothills.

Fiddletown 1 October 2009

* *1.68*

It blew hard all day while rain with leaves flew across a battered landscape while the first storm of the season swept across valleys, hills and mountain tops. Then the harvest begins its conclusive phase.

Today I see hundreds of walnuts strewn among limbs of trees and debris of foliage. Nothing but time and work will straighten this frightful mess.

......

Days begin with darkness inside or outside the house walls vanishing behind invisible screens send messages floating within that spread anxious melancholy or foreknowledge of finite time then the world populated by inaudible whispers contracts to a point that was not and that cannot be just is such as when it vanishes its absence is unnoticed and un-mourned

......

I gather remnants of life scavenger with purpose but without future thus the endeavor becomes purposeless purpose driving the balance of time like small irreversible tide the crimson tide tinted silver by moonlight as it wells up nocturnal obscure fauve

......

Friends reach to each other across a divide greater than distance; one finds that either hermetic or open, the experience remains uncertain if two separate life experiences can be bridged satisfactorily. Thus one will wonder after a long conversation whether the next opportunity of communication will be halting or deprived of interesting subjects. Nevertheless one should try to maintain those fragile connections even at the expense of altering perceptually the remembered past.

Fiddletown 14 October 2009

* *1.69*

Burgundy-red pyramid of foliage highlights the sunlight in the morning all that is now the foliage of a Seckel pear tree recalling festival days and ruddy faced pears hanging like ornaments. The translucent leaves glowing patches of color an invisible hand has painted on the canvas of nature tomorrow will diminish and eventually cover the earth that fed them with a brown-gray mantle. Behind glass I gaze out beyond the red hills at the chill of a late autumn morning.

Fiddletown 4 November 2009

* *1.70*

A time tunnel connected Fiddletown to the world that in the past was home for decades. Speeding through the great California valley the car carried us swiftly from home to home even when you know there is no home anywhere.

The room is not ready, time is useless, patience sooths fatigue as we discover Christmas already in the retail shops. We move personal effects, fruit tray, wines and other produce two flights up. The motel suite is as it was in the last visit; with a little more wear but comfortable for a week of visiting friends in S. California.

Pasadena and Altadena look untouched by the economic downturn, hardly any houses are up for sale, everything is in good repair and the shops we visit are busy with customers.

You have left and yet you have not, one eye seeing now and the other then without knowing which are which, passively recounting events that unrelated references recall.

......

Traffic in S. Lake is heavy as we pull by the Del Rio residence; fifteen years ago it seemed considerably quieter. At the door Domna in black dress and gold choker, Arturo stands behind her as both look remarkably well after a year and a half of all kinds of struggles.

Later at a French bistro of S. Pasadena we discuss life events and recollections of the past while finishing off a bottle of Côtes du Rhône. Well past ten at night we return to their home and then to our temporary one. Oliver no longer waits for them by the kitchen door and his protégé Baby is somewhere in N. California beginning a new life.

Pasadena 8 November 2009

* *1.71*

Sunday dawn cauldron of noise now unexpected like wake-up alarm is effective in stirring me up from the lethargy of dreams. Through the curtain the streaming light foretells a clear sky and a mild day urging me to rise.

Later while driving to Whole Foods for breakfast we know that lunch has been canceled because of Larry's sudden illness. The market has added more counters with prepared food and tables and chairs following the trend of people relying on ready-made meals for sustenance. Are we to be witnesses someday supermarkets that fill their shelves mostly with ready to consume products?

The coffee counter has been moved to a different location and is consolidated with the juice bar. I seek the muesli and raisin rolls at the shelves nearby selecting three for breakfast. The plans for the day are developed over a cup of mediocre latte.

....

On the south side of San Pasqual Street near S. Lake, where a large and mostly empty parking lot used to be, with messy ivy growing on the pedestrian walk and a palm tree that regularly dropped fruit, a new and pretentious complex of flats rises. To open on December 9 this year, it will contain courts, pool, garden and other amenities that aim to cater to high-living individuals. We hear that prices start at $1.7 M for flats starting at 1,000 and go up to 3,000 sq. ft. Next to the complex the apartments that graced the street for decades are dwarfed though the old oaks still dominate.

The Borders store on S. Lake has a reduced selection scattered all over its two floors. Thus we meander with minimal results. After catching a movie, Vroman's is an oasis of interesting books, even though to my memory not as good as it used to. As we walk through the streets of Pasadena, I am impressed by the growth of apartment complexes of mixed use and of their scale and girth. The city is no longer quaint, it exudes urbanity from every pore and its inhabitants are suburbanites in search of an upscale city. I find it attractive but no longer enticing as it used to be a couple of decades ago.

....

Green Street at night is oddly very animated. Malbec, an Argentine restaurant that opened its doors a couple of years ago is filled with people. Dan and Nilda are seated, we join them. They look good, they look older. The baton of life is passed to their son who finishes his undergraduate studies. Wine fuels talk but the quality of food disappoints us. Why is it now restaurants have no distinct cuisine and consistent quality? Later we get involved in cabalistic discussions with Nilda, the best I can describe any futile arguing over the content of life and claimed truth.

We walk out of an empty restaurant past 10:00 PM which would have been too late for Pasadena of yore.

Pasadena 9 November 2009
❊

* 1.72

The Caltech campus is a favorite place for strolling and discovering what changes have taken place since the last visit. This time we are overwhelmed by the metamorphosis. Nearly every building has been remodeled; the grounds modified and new buildings rising reshape the perception of the place. This is a different environment than the one I have known and lived for almost fifteen years in the 60s and 70s.

The former Booth Computing Center now renamed Powell-Booth Laboratory for Computational Research has been radically reshaped inside, my visual memory still recognizes certain transformed areas and the stairs. The large machine room where once mainframes and other large computers hummed is now a maze of offices and conference rooms. The second floor lit by new skylights accommodates a comfortable periodical library that has taken the space of the offices of Dr. McCann and of the Computing Center's management. The space extends to the east in the form of corridor to the Jurgensen building and conference area that has taken the place, among other things, of my old office. Yet the interior has been redone with great taste and obviously at great expense as the new additions in the campus show.

All paths in campus lead to the Athenaeum from which the olive tree walk issues west to link with the library, rising above a pond of water. The shaded courtyard of the Athenaeum is being prepared for some event by staff members who place settings and flowers on the tables. In such serene environment pettiness and ambitions seethe just below the surface.

Along the garden area camellia japonicas prepare their spring blooms while low-spreading Sasanqua camellias in bloom already herald the advance of winter. By the pond we sit to gaze at one of the oldest oak trees in California as the fountain surges and ebbs in the pond.

....

On Allen St. we find a small Armenian restaurant for lunch. We are the entire clientele of a mother-daughter team. It feels quiet and withdrawn away from the bustle of the center.

....

I walk through the Old Town streets looking around, trying vainly to place myself here. My habits and the city's surroundings have changed too much. It would be impossible to leisurely walk and browse in S. Lake Ave. on Saturdays, as my habit had been of several years.

....

Dinner at Azeen's Afghani Restaurant concludes with rosewater/cardamom/nut custard that is superb. At the parking structure there are no longer cashiers for paying, they have been replaced by a machine that accepts credit cards...

Pasadena 10 November 2009

1.73

They live in the heart of change, where Pasadena becomes more alien with its new architecture, large complexes and traffic snarled streets, yet their flat retains its old flavor, their life its unruffled tempo and blend of old and contemporary that is their hallmark.

We walk down the streets with them to the renovated Pasadena Railway Station which houses a restaurant and bar. Gus talks about his trip to see his family in Slovenia, the people, the places and events. His thick mane now thin gives him an air of child. From Pasadena to New York by train, New York to London by ship and then by train again to his village that the Germans called Klein Sontag and has changed its names many times, a long trip much the way they used to be before flying.

Seated outdoors in semi-darkness, talking, eating and sipping wine we experience the noise of a city close up, the rumbling trains, helicopters and speeding vehicles with wailing sirens. And the city grows to a larger jungle of steel, concrete and indifferent people.

Back inside their flat we see old Bogie struggle with his blindness and partial deafness to keep up with Gigi and still be part of his family that both dogs have been members of for almost seventeen years. Gus again spends time in assembling Leica cameras. Maria is about to embark in digitization of their photo negatives. We talk about Leica cameras like we used to years ago.

When we return to the motel the streets are almost empty. Outside its center, Pasadena still retains some of its old flavor.

....

Corfu is now half Mexican and half Greek restaurant, an odd culinary combination. John and I sit across from each other talking by the bay window. Age starts to show but he is full of gossipy enthusiasm and humor, about family, friends and life. ARCO hardly comes up during our time together, just on the sidelines like an old prop. How strange, I think, we have remained friends for so many years...

....

A belt and a hat is all we wanted to buy; we walk out of SEARS with a belt and three shirts, late for our appointments and laughing. Breakfast was so disappointing again and with only two multigrain rolls. In relatively clear air the mountains are visibly hardly touched by the fire above Altadena, yet the fire months old still has hot spots at inaccessible places...

Pasadena 11 November 2009

✣

* *1.74*

Mostly cloudy over S. California which alters the mood by tinting images gray and infusing air contaminants liberally. In Huntington Gardens a crowd waits patiently at the gates for the noon opening. The place must have looked stunning once in the light of San Gabriel Mountains. To be merciful to oneself one has to wear the spectacles of the past for seeing what is not there today, places, people or oneself.

The Rose Garden Tea Room is packed with people who drink their tea in small cups and consume delicately small and tasteless sandwiches, salads, petit fours and tarts. Chatting fills the time while the tea becomes astringent and the public invisible in the midst of hurrying waiters.

....
The muesli rolls at Whole Foods are more numerous today but smaller while the fresh milk latte tastes surprisingly better. Phone calls, daily planning and recalling instances of conversations with friends occupy every moment of the morning breakfast...

....
With the room still unmade we have to spend time elsewhere. We drive to Costco in Duarte to see what TV sets are available, weaving in and out of traffic and streets with Emily's assistance.

....
The President Thai has renovated its dining room but neglected its food that is bland and undistinguished. With Rodanthi the talk turns to her illnesses and medications she takes. How she has been transformed by time and her nemesis illness. More bland tea accompanies dinner. The night is haunted by light haze...

Pasadena 12 November 2009

* 1.75

Sprinkles on the windshield scatter reflections of automobile lights as the car turns on Lotus Street approaching the motel. It is not quite the promised rain just a sign that seasons are about to change in the Southland.

Late again for a weeknight, this time in Il Fornaio, we witnessed the gradual closing down of the restaurant as the customers departed little by little. Elaine and Erika had to share an entire evening's worth of recollections and companionship. The food and wine though not exceptional were pricey but kept us going all the while.

At the parking lot it was necessary to use the credit card for exiting...

....

At the Pasadena Library's periodicals reading room someone snores slumped on one of the leather armchairs, someone who probably is homeless and depends on the tolerance of the institution for survival. I thumb through a magazine waiting for Elaine who is visiting a former colleague. I cannot warm up to the environment; perhaps it always felt not so intimate and a bit over worn by public use. Now all faces have become unfamiliar, a process that repeats over and over when re-visiting former haunts.

....

Through the arches against the sunlight the City Hall of Pasadena looks splendid. In the interior garden only one older oak tree remains, one fell recently and several replacements are growing around the tall fountain of lion heads regurgitating streams of water. Across the street to the east the promenade leads to the hotel Westin formerly Double Tree.

At her face I see the ghostly image of Adolfo who has been gone for several years now. If it were not for a photograph I took in the 70s and which is placed in one of the albums perhaps his face and memory would have faded, yet this photo has captured the beauty of our friends' youth at a moment of folly. Our inner eye still sees them as such.

....

Crisp multigrain raisin rolls with steaming frothed milk and coffee, the breakfast of visitors to Pasadena. How do I miss our quiet breakfast at home and the light of the Sierra Foothills...

Pasadena 13 November 2009

* *1.76*

From the window the mountains show clearly under cloudy skies and a breeze is swaying the fronds of the palms. By the time we step into the car the sun discreetly shows and patches of blue alter the celestial landscape of a cool day.

....
On Arroyo Parkway to downtown L.A. the traffic is slower because of congestion and comes to a crawl as we enter downtown with all its freeway interchanges. In spite of progress in public transportation the volume of vehicles is higher. I fall in step with the pulse of traffic surging now in the direction of Santa Monica while I recall countless times I drove this stretch of freeway.

On Cloverdale we exit to surface streets merging in a different traffic pattern that moves in constrained city byways. Everywhere one lane is taken by parked cars except for 10th Street which is very wide. There the apartment building we lived in forty years ago still stands with a minor facelift. Everywhere in Santa Monica, particularly south of Wilshire Blvd new apartment complexes have taken the space of small homes or duplexes.

The building on 1025 Colorado stands quietly vacant; day laborers still wait hopefully for a prospective employer. The empty parking lot, a rare occurrence in this city, is in good repair. It is not too long of a wait until a postal employee shows up to let us and Chris in the building. While looking over the ravages of fifty years of Post Office tenancy I have nostalgic remembrances of our youth in Santa Monica, those uncertain and troubled times and its fog shrouded summers.

....
Driving on Wilshire Blvd heading east towards downtown is an aggravating experience but worth it for the memories it brings back and a glimpse of quintessential Los Angeles.

....
Erika and Mary are waiting in Azeen's that is all booked up. Instead we will dine at Yugene Kang's in the proximity. Mary talks about their life of the last decade or so and of her travel to

Cuba; the wine flows easily, the night stretches out, the restaurant is comfortable. We part again late into the evening.

Pasadena 14 November 2009

* *1.77*

Apex of the S. California visit this Saturday that commences the conclusion of the trip adds quite a few miles to the automobile odometer by successively driving to Claremont and to Irvine from Pasadena. The sense of loneliness and alienation rises inside the cabin of the car as one accelerates through the freeway system, part of the speeded up mass of cars moving through time and space at random. Everything appears familiar and out of context at the same time, life transformed to disjointed memories threatens itself with probability.

Friends who wear late age masks reflected on our tired eyes welcome our visit like an overdue comet arrival. One must be uncertain of such visitation as our ages reach the upper limits. We remember to forget and converse to remember, all in good humor and jest.

Finally in bed past midnight we prepare for a short night's sleep with thoughts of imminent travel.

Pasadena 15 November 2009

* *1.78*

Leaving Pasadena with a mild Santana blowing palm fronds and clear skies we drive towards the desert. The steady traffic at times becomes heavy even when we reach Barstow. Distant hills and mountains bathed in violet color soften a harsh landscape. One can lose all reference in this scrubby flat landscape seemingly void of life.

Adelanto looks like a depressed town on the edge of civilization as the wind sprays sand on dilapidated shacks scattered throughout vaguely defined yards with occasional phthisic trees.

Emily guides us to the house where Francisco and Rosie live. He is tinkering with the engine of the truck that he has trouble with. The house, one low story is in unfinished state, with its core only furnished. He has not had steady employment for quite some time and it shows.

He and I busy ourselves with solving the mystery of the converter box, tweaking controls and securing the antenna on the roof. We conclude the converter is defective before heading out to lunch to a nearby Mexican restaurant. Daniela, their daughter comes with us, a charming two and half year old girl. On the way we listen to their woes, each from the other person. Sad story, we feel sad for them, for decisions mistakenly taken.

Lone Pine 16 November 2009

* *1.79*

During the darkest part of the year thoughts become opaque hiding their true nature from their creator, like birds take to gathering in flocks and obscuring the few blades of grass that timidly cover muddy hills. Will tomorrow be there to greet a rising sun from the depths of lost memories?

Fiddletown 15 December 2009

* *1.80*

Descriptions of an alien world, how interesting would that be to a reader, rather than a different exposure of a familiar theme? Reading Proust over a long period and in short doses has become a pleasure I look forward to.

Last night a holiday dinner did not add much to the sense of season. As I sat listening when I was not talking about Greece with another guest, I had to refrain from making remarks. Smart dog retired to his sleeping cot after the appetizers were over. Outside the sky was dark perhaps preparing to rain. We drive through the forest where nothing seems familiar or hospitable; soon house lights make their appearance, human settlements are all around.

      Fiddletown 16 December 2009

* *1.81*

Doubt and self-examination reduce one's ability to enjoy the transitory state of life. Remembrances of happy moments merge with shadows conjured by the persistent investigation even if the intent is to intensify awareness of the road that led to the present position in one's development. Cast out all preconceptions to accept all information without filters that reject and select from the massive flow is an unattainable proposal. To seek oneself one must eliminate interference from unacceptable sources. How can this be achieved?

      Fiddletown 27 December 2009

Chapter 2. West to East

2.01

A new decade of the 21st Century has begun for anyone who tracks the passage of time in this fashion. I count it as my seventh decade on this planet, one of the billions of humanoid life forms enclosed in the cocoon of destiny common to all forms sharing earthly quarters. And though we perceive the inexorable fatal terminus in a common effort look for an escape we intuit absent.

The cycle of things is visible in the farm urging me to resume repeating practices for the season and as weather moves the timeliness forward, I feel the need to begin pruning trees as soon as possible.

Fiddletown 4 January 2010

2.02

During the night it rained in short intervals, forming images to go along with cascading dreams. I grasp what is undefined attempting to weave a page of descriptions that do not match the vision, just traces left behind. Who is to vouch of the accuracy of the original image created without colors, sounds or symbols? The image that directly applied itself on the sensory complex of the subconscious, like a breeze rustles selected leaves of the foliage.

The tree roots have invaded the vegetable garden and now a fight has begun. Primal shapes entwined in the soil strangle and choke other life, struggling for space, water and nutrients. I upset the balance in favor of my goals, unfairly and humanly.

Fiddletown 11 January 2010

* 2.03

Carelessness caused by anxiety or ennui? What drove me to instigate situations that might have injured me gravely? The second summer of the military duty I contrived to pose as target for a revolver loaded with a single bullet, which Margaritis believed to be blank despite my warning. I moved just in time to see a hole on the white wall at the height of my head and Margaritis' stunned face staring at the smoking gun. A couple of months later I decided to experiment with rocketry; having surplus explosives in store I launched an empty missile to vertical ascent from the creek on the border of the military camp. It landed in the park of the village; fortunately no one was strolling there at the time and with the regimental HQ staff being away nothing was reported. Later the restructuring and relocation of the regiment kept me working overtime until the move from Methoni to Polykastron was accomplished. Almost half a century away I still experience the shock and see images of my folly.

    Fiddletown 13 January 2010

* 2.04

Sunlight surprises me and delights me with its advance on the wall of the guest bedroom; already its geometric patterns frame the headboard of the bed presaging the coming of spring... I prepare to resume tasks that the rainstorms have interrupted.

    Fiddletown 27 January 2010

* 2.05

Perfect memory does not befall fragments flotsam floating in the sea of oblivion where shipwrecked souls gather despairing for lifejackets the prey of a little dogfish without master

Fiddletown 24 February 2010

2.06

I spent hours looking for a solution to a problem that probably is my ineptitude in using the micro keyboard of the Smartphone, finding neither solution nor an acceptable replacement for the Moto Q. The day brings good and bad news from friends in Greece, news that make it clearer that a trip is essential.

Fiddletown 25 February 2010

2.07

How then does it come to be morning after darkness?
Fair Oaks 18 March 2010

2.08

Last minute details become pressing, a SIM for the phone to give access to business back home at reasonable rates, an extra battery to allow longer periods between charges but most of all good humor which is harder to find. The time is near for the journey to Greece and Sicily, the joy lagging behind.

Fiddletown 27 March 2010

2.09

I wait over a cup of coffee for the car to be serviced. The weather has turned wintry again, threatening with rain and snow even though we have entered spring. Uncertainty and worries besiege us in the New Year that has brought not totally unexpected conflict.

Nearly a decade later since my first visit to this Honda dealership, I realize the many changes that happened. The surroundings have changed as result of the building frenzy of the recent past though still one can get a glimpse of the Sierra's magnificent snowcapped peaks. The venerable Canyon oak in front of the dealership holds sway and reigns over cold or hot days. Man is humbled by the longevity of Nature and its persistence, when contemplating his own rapid decline and loss of remembrance. Since the tomorrow has become even more uncertain than the long term future it adjusts one's outlook with a broad brush of impermanence.

The coffee shop is busy, busier than it has been for the last two years. Slowly the economy is picking up from its deep recession. I sit facing toward the city, seeing the mountains only with my inner vision and feel grateful...

Shingle Springs 2 April 2010
❧

* 2.10

The first hop is over; the rest of the continent and then an overnight hop of the Atlantic as we travel eastbound. Rise before 3:00 am to catch the shuttle to the airport, rise to meet the sun before its time. The cups on the counter wait for milk and they are nectar for the sleep-deprived.

The shuttle is already waiting at the gate at Primrose. In the night darkness the driver drives comfortably through the freeways through Sacramento to the airport. Every major journey now begins here and ends here. As airports go Sacramento is a hustle-free, provincial backwater airfield.

Washington Dulles Airport, 14 April 2010
❧

* 2.11

Forty one years ago the Munich Airport was a fraction of the expansive and comfortable complex it is today. Gray morning as the airplane lands safely to disgorge its cargo of passengers and their gear. Spring has not yet taken a foothold in Bavaria. Through bleary eyes it is a comforting picture however, the final stage of a multi-leg itinerary that has proven a no-frills flight. Avarice or desperation drove airlines to that level of reduced service? United has reached new lows making likely they will adopt such measures as those made already by small inter-European carriers..

Next step our flight to Thessaloniki with Aegean Airways.

Munich Airport 15 April 2010

❧

2.12

Aegean Airways is a refreshing change in today's world of airlines, serving an elegant lunch and beverage on a 1 hour 40 minute flight. The hostesses are courteous, pleasant, pretty, young and fashionably dressed. Before long the plane is landing at Macedonia Airport, on the outskirts of Thessaloniki. The old airport is just sufficient for the low volume it handles and it seems barely maintained.

Sissy waits for us in the hall along with other people also expect the arrival of someone dear; with her is Ilias who drives us to her home. In the gray overcast light everything looks unattractive. Traffic moves with purpose but less order, clumps of traffic form at interchanges of the Peripheral Road. Ilias is visibly distracted by life changes, his wife who had surgery for thyroid condition is generally in poor health; their daughter from Chicago and her child moved in with them after her divorce and their son who lived in N. Carolina has just made a major career and lifestyle move…

The structure obstructing the views of Sissy's place is to our left as we drive by on the lower street and the multistory building bulges out, dominating the surrounding space. Soon we are inside the warmth of the home and we settle down.

Harry comes in after a day of performing three surgeries, no doubt tired but not visibly subdued while he participates in our conversation about their lives and kids.

Fatigue hangs heavy on our eyelids in spite of a large cup of coffee. We must persist until late evening hours to avoid jet lag and every effort we make brings us one step closer to the desirable goal. After dinner Elaine retires to bed while I check the result of software updates in Sissy's notebook. Not receiving business news from Santa Monica today could be both good and bad.

Thessaloniki 15 April 2010

2.13

Night hangs about for a long while with pale ghosts of vague light; sleep was disturbed from cats wailing somewhere nearby. Occasionally a car sped by caused the left eyelid to open a bit; nonetheless it was still the same shapeless night. When daylight came suddenly bursting from under the drapes it felt like the beginning of an infinitesimal world.

Quiet throughout all floors of the building; both Sissy and Harry have left for work. A note on the dining table reads - *I am sorry I did not explain where things are*...yet everything is ready on the table and fetching anything else is very easy. Sunlight drapes the edge of the table, a welcome passing visitor. Around a pot of hot coffee we recollect the night.

In Sissy's office, the morning is spent doing e-mail, computer tuning and planning. Having a follow-up proposal for the lease, Elaine reviews and writes her comments in response to the company's. The weather remains cool, foggy and unstable though there is no precipitation. Leonidas rises late to dress and go out to the "University". When Sissy and Harry return from work we sit down for lunch to find out that Harry has secured five tickets to Charis' Alexiou recital (for three of us and Mina and Dimitri.)

In the late afternoon we visit Anna and Vassilis, both shadows of their former selves. Anna maintains her sweet expression and endearing manners that remind me of so many happier times, yet one is quite conscious of how aware she is of her frailty. Vassilis has shrunk and looks his illness, which he tries to hide. No one knows what goes on in his tangled mind, the pain, suffering and now the sense of rapid deterioration. Petros, friend of family and of Vassilis is here to take him for a walk; off they go in the waning light of the late afternoon.

-

It has been a gray winter and spring that invaded my inner space, covering memories with the fine dust of time. I long for summer and resurrection of nature even though I know it to be so separated from the past.

-

The sold-out Alexiou recital begins with pictures of Athens and Thessaloniki under the siege of loud orchestration. She still has a strong voice except it has lost some gracefulness and subtlety. The audience is transfixed; she loves adoration and pours out her soul. The musicians that accompany her are very good even if a bit too energetic and loud.

It takes us awhile to exit the parking area; Dimitris and Mina seem tired and decline Sissy's invitation for supper. It is already past midnight and they have to drive to their country home.

Thessaloniki 16 April 2010

❦

* *2.14*

Thessaloniki has grown to a megalopolis extending from eastern shore to the western side of the Thermaic Gulf, draping over hills and spreading far afield. Around this neighborhood three-story apartment buildings (some illegally four or five) replace more graceful older multi-story houses with gardens.

We jump on the minibus of Line 15, an efficient speeding devil, to the heart of the city. Everything we pass by, buildings, squares, parks, cemeteries and groups of people, are entwined by speeding traffic shapes, a modern version of Laocoon and his sons strangled. I recognize and I do not recognize this landscape, which continues to be colorless under gray skies.

At the White Tower, Sissy checks its hours of operation. Yes, it will be open tomorrow to visitors; today's crowds are pouring out its entrance. We will begin our promenade then by the Hall of Music, at the eastern end of the port, where a public quay framed by a park begins and winds its way to the White Tower. There it joins the old quay that skips along the main port.

We share tales of our lives as we walk or stop to sit at one of the benches, an opportunity for me to call our friends in Larissa; walking leisurely we become part of a scene that could be in one of Angelopoulos' movies.

-

Sissy's planned gyros lunch is postponed; the restaurant located in Diagonios is closed on weekends or holidays. Instead around the corner an upscale *ouzeri* becomes our refuge. The menu includes a tempting selection of fish that we order accompanied by a small carafe of *tsipouro*. The quality of food is uneven as is the service, yet we manage to enjoy it because of the camaraderie. *Tsipouro* weighs heavily on the eyelids and our cousin who spent her morning chairing a conference on diabetes is the most affected.

-

Late nap makes for late evenings, one that I spend trying to clean up (in vain) Leonidas' notebook computer from a bevy of malware. Afterwards I realize it must be a dream laboratory for anti-malware developers. I hope the malware don't come to haunt me in my dreams tonight...

                   Thessaloniki 17 April 2010

* *2.15*

*P*edro *the Peruvian dog snapped and played keenly as no other animal could do, the dog with elongated snout and upright ears. He is just a mythical creature, an expression that was* *preserved for no reason at all. Pedro is somewhere in my inner memory sleeping and waiting for his turn to harass me.*

Morning, the elevator behaves strangely, the light of day promises little relief from overcast skies, just like gloomy weather in S. California during the month of June. Toast, honey and marmalade accompanied by coffee fortify us for a day of visiting museums.

The first visit is at the Modern Museum of Art (Τελλόγλειο Ίδρυμα Τεχνών) by the University followed by the White Tower in the esplanade at the port. Ancient Drama and Opera related arts exhibits fill the first floor; higher floors contain a National Bank of Greece collection of 20th Century Greek *plein-air* painters and the historic material about the 1965 Biennale of Sculpture in Athens. An actress/singer in the second floor performs vocal musical exercises, theater and oration. Children roam around with family members on their Sunday outing.

On the way to the Tower it rains lightly. There is a waiting line but the wait is short. In the interior a permanent multimedia exhibit of Thessaloniki›s history occupies multiple floors. The sun makes a weak appearance when we reach the top of the Tower, enough to highlight a magnificent landscape in all sides.

-

Harry spends many hours keeping us company, more than in all those previous visits. What has happened to modify his behavior -- family dynamics or age could account for it. Sissy works hard in the office, labors at home taking care of her entire family and is a wonderful hostess to us.

-

Later in the evening we go to the movies in the suburbs to view *Ghost Writer*; the Cineplex is comfortable and luxurious inside a shopping mall, much like the U.S. Sissy receives a call from her mother near the end of the movie. Lana, her home care assistant, had to leave for the evening and left Anna without assistance. Crisis upon crisis weigh heavily on her shoulders.

Thessaloniki 18 April 2010
❖

2.16

Rain! Through wet streets we descend to the small *bougatsa* shop for breakfast of coffee with cheese and spinach *bougatsa*. Over a cup of hot coffee looking out at the people passing with their umbrellas, small trucks unloading supplies and the rain lashing the pavement, we feel defeated with the plans for today. Yet within half hour the hard rain abates and we leave Stelios's shop for the city center and the White Tower where the Cultural Route Bus begins a historical tour of the city.

At 11:05 the terminus is empty, rainwater drips from the shelter roof. Has the bus left or it has fallen behind schedule because of rain and traffic? We wait fifteen minutes, not having anything else to do on a cool rainy day. In spite of my pessimism the bus arrives and pulls up to load the next wave of (two) sightseers. Thus it ends to be a private tour of the historic areas of the city, supplemented with explanations from the young woman who handles the tickets. The most evocative quarters are those of the Upper City, composed mostly of single or double story houses clinging on steep hills and accessible by way of narrow streets. The city's defensive walls can be seen here and there for short spans until one reaches the *Heptapyrgion*, which still retains much of its old structure. The bus begins to climb down completing its loop at the White Tower.

Everything is still wet as we step down and head towards the Rotunda just a few steps off Hadrian's Arch. To no big surprise the place is locked up, leaving us the only possible alternative, walk around it and peek through the wrought iron fence.

The Church of Acheiropoiitos is also in the vicinity and it is locked as well. Only cats seem to have a free pass throughout antiquities and churches.

We hope that Sissy could meet us at the Diagonios Bar for gyros that she pined for so much. It is already 14:30, most of the faithful clientele is settling in. We order beer, salad, appetizers and gyros with fries. The phone rings, Sissy is calling to tell us she is just leaving the office. We will not share lunch today.

When we return we find Sissy and Harry having their lunch. We spend the evening at home.

  Thessaloniki 19 April 2010

❦

* 2.17

We wake up early in the morning to unfamiliar sounds. Doors slamming, objects being wheeled around, unloading of containers; it is the weekly Farmers' Market that is setting up in the street. Today the sun is out, the blue sky meets the sea far away and no one can exactly say if that hazy band is sea or sky.

After a swift breakfast we run down with Sissy to help with her shopping and to gape at all the abundant fresh produce. We must hurry because Dimitris and Mina are arriving to take us all for a day's excursion to East Macedonia and Thrace.

-

The car now speeds on new Via Egnatia to Philippi and even though we have been to it two years ago I find little I recognize. There has been additional building along the highway, invading previously agricultural spaces. At Philippi Dimitris parks the car and we walk to the entrance of the archeological site. Fleecy clouds descend from the mountainsides to greet us and to play in the infinite azure space that rises above the broken marble columns. The theater retains its acoustical qualities that enchant everyone. The site is extensive; I take an ascending trail toward the distant acropolis that is barely visible on the ridge and I am rewarded with a bird's eye view of the site. Where was it that the battle of Philippi took place, the battle that determined the future of Imperial Rome?

The River Nestos' Gorge, a natural preserve is nearby and definitely not to be missed. A modest hike by the river offers beautiful views and the opportunity to observe the flora of the place.

Having found ourselves in a location that places the town of Xanthi as the best alternative for having lunch, Dimitris drives on to Xanthi rather than return to Kavala. At a local's recommendation we lunch at Palaia Poli Restaurant whose specialties have a distinctly Oriental feel. As we leave the restaurant a brief shower bestows on the town a different edge, something very provincial and remote. Xanthi is renowned for its Oriental patisseries, an opportunity which we miss not!

It is a good half hour to Kavala if you do not get confused entering the main highway, which we do. Kavala is built on steep slopes like a Greek Theater around its naturally protected harbor. Well restored and preserved old buildings demonstrate a past of wealth, which is now restored through tourism. A walk to the city's ramparts opens magnificent views of the sea and the not so distant island of Thasos.

Much later we return to Thessaloniki where we arrive well into the evening.

Thessaloniki 20 April 2010

* 2.18

A bad cold seizes me next day. I felt it coming during the night hours. I linger longer in bed and stay at home to fight the infection. Since I can do a few things such as repair infected with malware computers, I spent a lot of time before a screen.

Thessaloniki 21 April 2010

* 2.19

From Thessaloniki to Larissa we take the train which is not affected by a Tempe rockslide. Ilias takes us to the train station by back streets to avoid blocked roads by demonstrating strikers. The train has no luggage car, we carry the suitcases aboard. The ride to Larissa is short where Thanos is waiting, having parked illegally. On the way to his house he speaks of more bad news. Explain

As always Argyro has prepared a feast for gods, only that this mortal feels the effects of a virus. I indulge drinking tsipouro, hoping it will cure me of the ills, but the best it does it helps me have a short siesta. I sweat profusely.

When everyone is up we gather the necessary belongings for a stay at Thanos and Argyro's house in Agia. When we arrive Argyro turns on the central heating and Thanos lights the fireplace. This old stone house, so lovingly restored, can be very cold and damp.

I stay in bed until dinner for which very thoughtfully Argyro has cooked soup, my favored *trahana*. As I eat I discover that I have lost my sense of smell; I can only taste bitter, sweet or sour. The wine that is poured I know to be treasured, it has been stored for many years; I nod approvingly while deeply regretting my inability to appreciate it.

   Agia 22 April 2010

2.20

Saint George is celebrated just half a block away at the eponymous church. Our friends have risen early to go to the services. In the half darkness of the room the sounds of the street intrude through the thick stone walls of the revived old house. One can picture faces, bodies immaterial, gesturing and talking through the stones of the river. How many people have wandered through the streets of the village in the passage of time? Nothing seems as severe as the isolation of a stone village.

Through the bathroom window a sunny day shows off the beauty of an azure sky which we have not seen for weeks. I hear the sound of steps and the turning of key on the entry door. Our friends are back and smiling. Breakfast; if I wish *trahana* I could have it. Instead I join in with coffee and cookies.

The Aghios Panteleeimon monastery on the border of Agia is manned by a few monks. In good repair, its stone walls enclose a peaceful courtyard with flowers and pesky cats. The monk who is present is welcoming but obviously had his tranquility interrupted. He opens the church and the refectory. Old frescos and icons look down at us in silence. And as good host the resident monk offers cold water and *loukoumia* to the guests; an offering of conciliation, we leave him in peace but not solitude since another monk and two lay men have arrived.

Throughout the mountain roads of Greece but particularly here in Mt Ossa peace reigns, vested in various hues of green. Thanos drives on, being familiar with the area, and stops at places to stroll and take photos. A white venerable donkey tethered at the side of the road munches philosophically on the fresh grass while waiting for the Angel of Death. What could I say to him that would be of solace, I don't even know any words for my own appeasement?

Kokkino Nero means Red Water, and red water is there for drinking and healing of all sorts of ailments. The water itself is clear but it leaves the bright color of iron oxide it contains. The main fountainhead is bright red. Like our water at home, only here it had many years of running from the same spring.

At Stomio by the sea we stop at a restaurant our friends patronize often. There I suffer quietly tasting little bites of different plates, mostly local fish. I cannot face up to *tsipouro* leaving Thanos without a drinking companion. To digest the lunch we walk to the farthest end of the village where the land rises to a promontory. The wind whips the sea and the trees of the land with equanimity. Wildflowers cling to the rocks and encroach in the sand. After searching for bits of beauty in the treasure storehouse we feel exhausted and take the road back to Agia.

Agia 23 April 2010

* 2.21

Meataxohorio, formerly Retsani, adjoins Agia on its northwest corner. Here young school children enjoyed the freedom of the countryside more than on half century ago, clambering over the boulders of the creek and munching on cherries. I have but a faint recollection of that, though the creek running through the village is surprisingly familiar. Walking around the center I am struck by the beauty of an inner garden filled with blooming roses. Its owner, a handicapped older man, happens to be nearby; he invites me in curious of my whereabouts.

A good cup of Mountain Tea under the pergola of the local Guest House and Restaurant brings me back to life. Sun streaming through vegetation keeps the chill of the breeze in check. The large old stone house is furnished exquisitely with period furniture. I would love to spend a week here during the summer.

Lunch is at a different place, again in Metaxohorio. Many plates stream to the table but little of the food finds its way to my plate. Abstinence from food reflects how I presently feel vis-à-vis the culinary world.

   Agia 24 April 2010

* 2.22

I spend our forty-fifth anniversary in bed trying to recover from the cold or flu that saps my strength. Later in the day the sun comes out, in time for our return to Larissa.

   Agia 25 April 2010

* 2.23

Torturous night with retching fits of coughing. I stumble blindly into an overcast day when I venture outside to purchase more medication. With Argyro taking care of a required smog inspection for the aging red FORD we sit quietly in the kitchen.

Thanos telephones at noon; he wants me to join him for business matters and tells me that he ran into Onik whom he informed of our visit. On the way I go by the main square to see him. There he sits alone at a table smoking a cigar impassively and looking at the passersby. Had I not seen his photo from 2007 I would not have recognized him. His expressionless face becomes animated when we make eye contact. He looks rather unkempt in his plaid flannel shirt, dark blue hunter's jacket and baggy pants. Baldness does not compliment his rotund face filled with gray stubble. He has not lost weight in spite of his medical condition and his family and business troubles. As we speak I discern the same person I knew years ago as he directs the discussion to the troubles of Greece, perhaps his attempt to reestablish the thread of fellowship long broken. When his son Nubar arrives I say my goodbyes.

-

In the afternoon we take a stroll in Larissa to see Anthi and later meet Giannis Molas. Anthi is surprised and happy to see us. During a little coffee break we chat about her family, the state of things in Greece and about us. I hear the words that become sounds, colors, shadows, I see the past as future and youth forgotten. Next block down is the only movie theater remaining from my childhood days, whose projector operator used to discard clippings of celluloid that were for us then such a trophy.

Near the main square we encounter a strange cortege of noisy motorcycles with young riders preceding the hearse. For minutes the enfilade slowly rolls disrupting traffic. The departed is one of their companions killed in the eve in a traffic accident.

Giannis willingly takes us to see the latest expansion of the Ancient Theater by the river. Meanwhile we catch up with news of a summer home he and Mary are building in his mountain village. We pass by Michalis Levi's shop where we visit a while until a coughing fit gets the better of me.

The Larissa visit has been too short and leaves me with a sense of deep frustration.

Larissa 26 April 2010

❋

2.24

Greece battered by the winds of adversity and all kinds of rumors is a dispirited place. The anger is rising against the political establishment, against their perceived lack of governance and increasing consensus that Greece has to sink or swim. There seem to be no optimists here to instill confidence and purpose. Thrown out to the lions or the Wall Street sharks by its friends is an accepted certainty.

-
I wait for Thanos' departure to say goodbye, I kept evoking scenes from our previous trips together and how time has turned. He had arrived home at 4:45 and he was preparing to leave by 8:30 for a court appearance at 9:00. We shake hands and promise to see each other again. Then back to bed I go coughing.

-
Argyro stays home, a taxi shuttles us to the train station where we check in the luggage and wait for the train to arrive. The Farmers' Market is just outside the station today, sending a stream of local shoppers through the main hall with bags full of fresh produce.

-
The train compartment is comfortable, clean and slightly worn though the car's exterior is covered with graffiti, visible from the inside on the window glass as patches of color and remains of some scraping.

-
Arriving in Athens, wait in the taxi line outside the train station for one hour. The subway is stopped because of a strike and we are caught between the taxi drivers' shift change and the busy hour of stores closing. People line up waiting in resignation and occasionally in good humor. Many try different venues for catch-

ing a cab, more than often unsuccessfully. We hold on to our luggage and our patience.

The taxi driver is business-like and drives to Varimbombi quietly and swiftly. Like most drivers he has been at this remote suburb only a few times, so I give him directions when we approach the Garas house. After unloading the luggage we ring the bell. We are expected and first to arrive is the dog Danny, bounding up to my chest with his tail flapping vigorously. Aimilia makes our arrival very welcome.

In the den we sip tea and have cookies shortly after, talking and waiting for Giannis to wake up from his nap. I feel my heart leap when he opens the door that leads to the upstairs and slowly makes his way to his now permanent chair. He is a smaller man, deeply bowed. It takes a while for his face to become animated. Thus we plunge again into conversation that had been left unfinished in our last visit. Or, is it a conversation we can never really end, one that is dealing with persons and faces from a common past?

We discuss the situation we face with our flight to Italy on the day that a general strike is scheduled and Aimilia's flight to London on Monday and we begin plotting next week. I make a reservation for Astor Hotel near Syntagma Square for Friday through Tuesday..

Varinbombi 27 April 2010

* 2.25

Next day finds us recuperating at Varimbombi. It is a cool windy day with fleecy clouds running across the sky. I spend time trying to assess our connectivity to the Internet, which turns out to be zero unless I use the phone. Then I spent most of my time reading Giannis' memoirs which he has been busy dictating to a lady who edits similar work. I find it warm and personal, sometimes detailed to excess and maybe overwhelming for someone who might not have a similar background.

-
Late in the afternoon Aimilia in vain drives us around Erithrea trying to locate an Internet Café. Ultimately her cousins, Andreas, a retired admiral and Pat, his English wife, offer the use of their Internet connection so that we may check Elaine's business e-mails. Andreas prepares his specialty tisane for coughs which I sip slowly while sitting in front of the keyboard. News is not good, confirming the "no news is good news" aphorism.

Varimbombi 28 April 2010

✤

2.26

The wind resumes in the morning, bringing back a biting chill. Nevertheless we visit the new Acropolis Museum that has received so much publicity. Photos are explicitly prohibited inside, shifting my attention entirely to the exhibits, the environment and my unpredictable cough. I find the wasted space and the discontinuity of the exhibits disturbing. Later when we will look toward Acropolis from above at the Astor Hotel, I will object to the architectural shape of the Museum itself.

-
I am still fighting an uncontrollable need to cough and the only remedy seems to be throat lozenges. When we retire to rest in the afternoon I call to change the day of the flight to Sicily. After almost an hour on a transatlantic call we succeed to move our departure a day earlier, on Tuesday. In the little time left I call friends to brief them of our plans and to find out how they are faring. The communication with Vassilis and Caterina is problematic due to the voice quality my special phone SIM delivers.

In the evening Giannis endures his excruciating pain to treat us to a night out at a *psarotaverna* in Erithrea. The variety and freshness of the seafood is remarkably high and the service very friendly. Tomorrow we will be leaving our friends for Hotel Astor in the Center of Athens. It seems like such a short stay…

Varimbombi 29 April 2010

* 2.27

Around noon with Aimilia on the wheel we return to Kifissia, once an oasis of green interspersed with small farms and large country homes for the privileged Athenians. Every available lot is undoubtedly going to be converted to an expensive multi-family structure incorporating green space. Many such projects are works in progress. Meanwhile more vehicles choke up the narrow streets of the center.

Under the awning of the outdoor café everyone is partially protected from the wind that continues to bend treetops and up-turn empty chairs. With gusts it sends up whirling puffs of pollen and dust that aggravate my cough. Yet the day is beautiful, the place comfortable and discussion flows freely until it is time to return for lunch.

Aimilia has prepared a delicious goat kid pot roast accompanied by salad, wine and the nostalgia of once again farewells.

-

The move to Astor Hotel takes place in the late afternoon. Giannis has phoned his regular taxi driver to drive us to Athens Center. We learn that the man's younger son of 23 has suddenly collapsed and died only a few days ago from unknown causes. Over a cup of coffee Giannis and Aimilia attempt to console the inconsolable father. Mr. Giannis cannot yet face the untimely separation, pursuing the cause of his son's death.

We leave in emotional chaos, thinking of the brevity of life as we embrace dear friends with whom we hope will meet again.

The traffic is heavy near the Athens Center and our driver takes side streets to avoid the worst congestion. People stream by, people you would recognize in different parts of the world, men with kaftans, long beards, blacks, Berbers, Chinese and shadows running along the walls of the neighborhood somewhere south between Piraeus and Athena's streets. This is the Kasbah of modern Athens.

In the hotel, familiarity and the same tired look of last year's renovation. Still it is a welcome spot in the center of Athens, a transit station to other destinations. It is almost one half century since I could have called this part home.

Expecting Giorgos Georgis to arrive in the hotel lobby is like waiting to meet oneself in the past. It is a curious feeling that I cannot get used to; still I look forward to the get-together.

With careful scrutiny I would have recognized him, to a great extent aided by his body movements, upright stand and his *komboloi* fingering. I wonder how he perceives me or if he would have recognized me in the street. Here we are forty five years later, strangers again. His wife Caterina and Elaine are chatting, getting to know a bit of each other while we sit at a table at the Bistro which has taken the place of Apotsos after it ceased its operations.

During our evening together Giorgos continues to astound me with memory capsules from the time we knew each other, remembrances that I have completely lost. Is memory then tied to locality, retained by everyday reminders in the form of subtle and mostly invisible messages?

The past is opened again to gaze at as we become familiar with each other's lives. We speak of ourselves, our environment and of Greece's current troubles. Late in the evening we take leave of the pretentious little Bistro and weave our way to Syntagma Square where we part, they to a northern suburb and we to our hotel.

Athens 30 April 2010

* 2.28

Daylight imparts brilliant Attic light and blue skies over Athens, something we have missed during this trip. After a late breakfast we take to the streets where people have begun to gather to celebrate the First of May and to demonstrate with speeches against the austerity measures. Syntagma Square has been reverberating with rousing Theodorakis' songs and Stadiou Street already is festooned with police. In the distance banners and chanting signal the arrival of the first wave of demonstrators.

In the direction of Acropolis quiet and song of birds suffuse the distant roar. While we sit on a bench of a tiny public park below the Rock of Acropolis we hear far-off the echoes of demagoguery. We follow the footpath below the ramparts to Propylaea. People promenade in front of closed gates among olive trees in full bloom and golden dry grass. In the gravel of the path a stunted dark green plant sends up a red poppy.

In the Hill of Philopappos many Greek families celebrate Πρωτομαγιά with picnics and gathering of wild flowers for the making of the traditional wreath. This stroll thus becomes a pilgrimage to our youth when we come upon the well where we had taken pictures of each other shortly after our first meeting. We take more photographs of another time with the immortal well, then visit the Philopappos' Monument at the crest of the hill. Below, city and sea simmer under the Attic sun.

Our lunch is visual more than culinary, the view of the Rock of Acropolis accompanied by ice-cream at the Dionysus Restaurant's loggia.

-

Alexandros arrives with Nana and Konstantinos to drive us in their car to Nea Philadelphia where the taverna *Η πόσις κα η βρώσις* is located on a small square. A mild evening outdoors, the company of friends and good food frame an early evening. Alexandros and his family need to attend the Triodion service for his departed mother tomorrow morning. Our return to the hotel is marred with an episode of violent coughing in their car.

Athens 1 May 2010

2.29

Observing a place involves latency and inertia not found in present day traveling. Much of our senses blunted by overstimulation or fatigue fail to offer the insights available to the unhurried pace of a serious traveler in the past. I now touch the surface of what exists without comprehension and leave a place taking with me regrets. Just as I rise in the morning I face the sight of Parthenon only seeing but not comprehending. Tomorrow separated by great distance I shall feel bitter regret.

-

Westward bound on Ermou Street, Ares and Lena Tzahanis with the two of us talk over the ills that plague modern Greece, the hyperbole of a situation I sought to escape when I left years ago. Ares is more subdued and a little depressed. I look at his face framed by white hair and hardly recognize the child I knew a long, long time ago.

A police car slowly rolls on the pedestrian walkway sending a number of African illegal vendors to flight. Watches, CDs, DVDs and purses get wrapped instantly in the sheet they have been displayed on and are hauled off a block away where another ad-hoc stall materializes. A way of life.

After Monastiraki we switch to Adrianou Street; there are crowds everywhere, people walking, shopping or eating at the sidewalk bistros and cafés and everywhere non-Greek street vendors hawk imitation or illegal copies of expensive ware.

Lena and Ares find the restaurant that has moved their dining area in an outdoor garden. We are squeezed in a corner among crowded tables with the few waiters literally running between the kitchen and the customers' tables. Lots of families celebrate May 1st in perhaps one of their last outings before the austerity measures hit home. The order is delivered in good time; the sausage and lamb ribs are exceptional.

Walking we return to Syntagma Square where we propose having a cup of coffee at the *Brazilian* a former haunt of writers and now of indifferent waiters and marauding pigeons. While sipping a latte a friendly pigeon takes to nipping my fingers expecting to find crumbs.

We accompany Ares and Lena to the Metro station and return to the hotel for a nap.

-

In a Sunday evening most eating places are closed. In the hope of finding home style cooking in a neighborhood less affected by tourism we head to Kolonaki where we had discovered a traditional style *taverna* in our last trip. *To Omorfon* is still there at the small square nestled higher up under Lycabettus on its north side. In a table outside three older men sit, who seem to enjoy each other's company with home-style food. Here I finally get to order a distinctive *bakaliaro plaki*, while Elaine discovers that the meatballs she orders taste very much like the ones we cook at home. When she does not finish her plate she requests a "doggie bag" that she means for one of the many stray dogs.

On the way back we cross Kolonaki Square at a quieter time but we find nowhere any of the usual stray dogs. It is a good thing the hotel room is equipped with a mini refrigerator. Tomorrow Monday we can expect more demonstrations, strikes and frenzied chatter on TV.

Athens 2 May 2010

✽

* *2.30*

Again under the Attic light, out of the window looms the Acropolis bathing in the morning mists. Further out, pollution gathers in layers and the throb of the morning traffic lulls the city. School boys on excursion from some island to see the antiquities are up early and have taken to clambering the stairs on their way to breakfast. This is the end of our morning leisure.

Finding our way to Theseion with a packet of leftover food for stray dogs, we traverse Ermou taking Mitropoleos to Monastiraki though we encounter no dogs as if they have magically entered a different time-space continuum.

We rest in front of Agia Marina whose original church dates back to 11th Century then we resume walking on the pedestrian walkway that leads to Acropolis.

Not far from there two stray dogs lie on the ground, not getting too roused by the food we offer. Finally both start to chomp it in a lazy sort of way; we conclude that they must have been recently fed.

From Acropolis we cross to Aiolou Street passing by the Tower of the Winds. Now we are in the heart of the old shopping district looking for light cotton nightgowns. Many of the old stores have closed down, victims of changing tastes and strong competition from large chains. With pleasure we purchase genuine Greek made cotton gowns and take our celebration to Desire for rest and refreshment. On route to our hotel room we stop at Ariston, just on the east side of the same block, to buy a couple of their special pita slices.

-

The luggage packed, bill paid, the remainder of the day is to be devoted to getting in touch with friends and tying any lose ends.

Athens 3 May 2010

❊

2.31

Today it is quiet around Syntagma Square but the car traffic is heavy. The taxi driver taking us to the airport tells us that everyone is trying to get their business done today before tomorrow's general strike paralyzes the country. From the open window the car fumes make my lungs burn slightly. At the east side of Hymettus there has been more urban sprawl. Although Markopoulo continues its wine tradition, Koropi has been so overrun by the airport expansion that its small wine output is sold only privately.

Our early arrival allows us the luxury of waiting without the anxiety of a cancelled flight. Down the long hallway a branch of Metropolis Records gives me the last opportunity to buy a DVD copy of Ψυχή Βαθιά.

-

The Alitalia flight crew is indifferent and almost uncivil. The company is insolvent and has not been successful in wooing a suitor for acquisition. Could its employees try harder to boost the image of the company or have they already thrown in the towel?

-

Fiumicino is visibly an aged airport and its mood blends with that of a gray sky. While we wait for the flight to Palermo I feel weak as if succumbing to this miserable cold anew. The airline changes the departure gate and later the departure time. Still we will be in our destination early in the afternoon.

-

From Palermo Airport the taxi shuttles us to the city by the coastal highway. Houses everywhere mark the increase in population and wealth of the area.

The Grand Hôtel des Palmes in the center of the city was a wealthy mansion that has been converted to a luxury establishment. Still I expected it to have a large garden; instead the building takes up the entire city block. The room is large and comfortable on the third floor with windows looking out to via Roma.

-

Finally we arrange to have a doctor examine us since we both have my coughs. Is it a case of Malade Imaginaire or one of Médecin malgré Lui? Dottore Roberto is a funny man whom we cannot communicate very well with. We all come to an agreement we are doing well, we get the required prescription and bill for medical services on the spot. He tells us he has been to medical school in the States, and then worked for NASA. How did he manage with such terrible command of the English language?

Afterwards we go out for our first contact with the city, in search of a meal. It has been a long day...

    Palermo 4 May 2010

❊

* 2.32

Palermo is an old city that wears its history on its sleeve, the decaying facades of buildings from many cultures and ages. Churches and palaces reflect sublimity and vanity of man through time. Throughout the more affluent part of the city center there is renovation in progress counterbalanced by the effects of neglect and auto pollution.

Walking south on via Roma glimpses of impressive buildings impress and delight the eye. In every street crossing you better be aware of anything that moves toward you, the motorcycles in particular. Confidence is the single most effective tool for a pedestrian navigating the chaotic streets of Palermo.

-

Piazza Marina by the port contains a few impressive Ficus Indica trees that have grown to huge proportions over centuries. One of the trees is pruned today with a large crane moving around a man with chainsaw. It is surrounded by palaces and churches from the time the Aragonese held sway here. Palazzo Abatellis is a city block away and the site where many Sicilian art treasures are exhibited.

A coughing fit seizes me ruining part of the visit to the art gallery. Afterwards we walk by the ramparts facing the port on our way to the International Museum of Marionettes, a delightful private museum with a huge collection of puppets and shadow puppets from the entire world.

Returning to the hotel we unwittingly make the wrong turn on via Roma that takes us to Piazza Julio Cesare where we stumble on the little Trattoria Trapani where we have a nice lunch and welcoming service. It takes us more than a few minutes to realize our mistake and turn around to catch via Roma at its start.

-

The first encounter with the group of people we will be travelling with takes place in the late afternoon. The tour leader Mariaelena Ciacci is charming, energetic and reminds us of Sissy. She invites everyone to join her at the suite allegedly Richard Wagner occupied when he was visiting Palermo. The suite has just been opened to the public by the hotel. I run out quickly when a coughing fit seizes me again.

     Palermo 5 May 2010

❁

2.33

The day begins with dark clouds drifting overhead, turning age-old gray and black walls darker, funereal almost. Maybe this day it will rain in Palermo. The city is unmoved as it goes about its daily business with the full orchestra of roaring vehicles, wheels screeching and the occasional wailing siren of ambulance or police vehicle.

-

The Regional Archaeological Museum is closed for repairs leaving us more time in our hands than we had planned. We proceed south to San Cataldo, Santa Maria del Amiraglio (La Martorana) and Santa Caterina. La Martorana is a gem in decay, at least externally. Many people crowd in its small space of diverse styles from different epochs. The gold leaf Byzantine mosaics with brilliant colors and austere lines dominate the later Baroque and Rococo frescos and overly ornate carvings. There among the ebb and flow of visitors it takes a minimum of concentration to be transported to a different world. Near the entrance there is a striking Byzantine mosaic which nearly everyone ignores. Christ anoints Roger I king:

ΡΟΓΕΡΙΟΣ ΡΕΗ ΙΣ ΧΡ

Several blocks due west are the remains of walls and the gate called Nuova Porta. To their southeast is the Piazza della Vittoria surrounded by il Palazzo dei Normani and several other palaces and churches. Many centuries of history sandwiched together deteriorate under the Sicilian sun while bathing in the fumes of motor vehicles. The square is dominated by a monument to Philip V to which time has been unmerciful. Sic Transit Gloria.

Rain starts to fall in earnest; we take refuge in the Cathedral that is flooded with crowds of visitors. Eventually under the protection of a cheap green umbrella we find our way back to the hotel.

-

I send an e-mail to inform friends that we have not been delayed by the unrest in Greece.

-

The tour group meets at 19:00 in the bar of the hotel. Mariaelena Ciacci offers a lot of useful information in her animated and humorous manner. Dinner follows at *Il Mirto e La Rosa* a nearby restaurant serving very good food. As usual an antipasto, pasta and a main course followed by dessert.

Palermo 6 May 2010

* *2.34*

Our last day in Palermo is rewarded with nice weather, sun and only few clouds. The tour program starts at 09:00 with Mariaelena introducing us to the local guide Laura, an informed and energetic woman whose sense of humor and strong personality remind us of Carmen.

For the second day in a row we visit the Cathedral and La Martorana discovering more details under the trained eye of Laura.

The next stop off point is the Palatine Chapel at the Palazzo dei Normani, a work undertaken by Roger II. Wonderful Byzantine mosaics, Arab inlaid stone work and Norman influence give the place splendor found only in Sainte Chappelle. The chapel has had the fortune to have been restored competently only a few years ago under the auspices of a German millionaire.

Afterwards we ramble in a subtropical garden to enter San Giovanni degli Eremiti constructed also by Roger II upon the remains of a previously built Benedictine monastery. There is something very peaceful to the stark simplicity of the interior which on the outside looks very Arabic with its round brightly colored domes.

-

After churches, comes the time for markets and the old food market of Baillaró is on our way. Fantastic amount of seafood piled high on tables is awaiting customers. Tuna and swordfish predominate giving a different view to one's feelings toward seafood. Lunch for the group is in a typical family trattoria in a Palermo neighborhood.

-

We spend afternoon at the Monreale Cathedral built in the 12th Century.

-

In the evening the two of us have supper at Il Scudiero, one of the places recommended by Mariaelena.

Palermo 7 May 2010

✣

* 2.35

Time to bid goodbye to the Grand Hôtel des Palmes and to turbulent Palermo. I yearn for the quiet of countryside even knowing that it is a contradiction to the soul of Sicily. The morning traffic is intense, slowing the bus progress to a crawl. Gradually the center peels away surrendering to the suburbs with more green space and equal lack of planning. Then the bus picks up speed and softly rocked side to side we are transported to the hillside where the remains of Segesta dominate the landscape. Fabrizio, the local guide, explains the arrangement of the temple.

By the stocky temple a deep ravine extends further out and then switches course towards the hills revealing a stream of water rushing through. It is reputed that in this chasm the Elymians threw convicted criminals.

-

Erice is a hill town whose charm has been spoiled by tourism. On the top of Mt San Giuliano, the walled medieval and later town is beset by winds and occasionally by fog. Erice's temperature remains moderate when the plain below is baking, making it very attractive to vacationers. Avoiding a big lunch we find a café and share the table with Norm, Carolyn and Jen. After lunch it is time to splurge on an almond confectionery.

-

Mazara del Vallo is a peculiar city that feels suspended between Europe and Africa. Similarly the weather experiences wide swings in temperature influenced by the prevailing winds. The hotel in which we stay, Mahara Hotel, is a converted *balio* now luxuriously revamped to Africanate style.

Mazara has a small new museum that houses one statue, an alleged Greek satyr discovered more than a decade ago in the sea and carefully restored. I try in vain to convince myself of its origins and the explanation given for the character represented.

-

Mariaelena leads us through small alleys to via Garibaldi and Main Square. From there later it is short walk to Alla Kasbah where we dine in very good fusion food, fusion between Tunisian and Sicilian cuisines.

Mazara del Vallo 8 May 2010
❊

* *2.36*

Mozia a main Phoenician post on the island of San Panteleo is mostly buried under the weight of millennia. Thanks to Joseph Whitaker a serious effort to explore its antiquities has been undertaken and a small museum with local findings has

been established.
The small distance from the mainland is crossed by a motor-boat. Our skilled guide Saverio ushers us through the museum and then leads the group on a hike of the island. An ancient manmade pond that was used to load and unload merchandise, still exists, landlocked now, a few yards from the shore. Far away the city of Marsala hugs the edge of the coastline

-

Because a marathon has closed the access to the place where a tasting of Marsala had been arranged, an improvised Marsala tasting takes place at the café that faces the island. This is followed by a sumptuous lunch at Maharah Hotel concurrent with a Confirmation celebration.

-

The afternoon finds us visiting the Gazzerosse Winery for tasting. The winery, still a fledgling, has set up a magnificent food spread for the guests. I spend most of the visit talking or rather listening to Salvatore di Gregorio, one of the partners and a likeable man.

Since our pace of eating in Sicily is excessive we decide to skip dinner tonight.

Mazara del Vallo 9 May 2010

* 2.37

From Mazara to Agrigento and the Valle dei Templi is a long and not very interesting ride. Sicily appears even more impoverished and dry than I had imagined and those flat scrubby valleys tire the eye so. Yet at one point when the road starts climbing, turning like a powerful snake through the hills, there is a change in the landscape, defined at first from the farthest hill covered by modern buildings. The modern city of Agrigento is a city that grew on top of ancient Ακραγας, a striking juxtaposition to the visible ancient Greek temple. Then as we approach we start seeing even more temples and ruins.

At the bus parking space we meet Luigi our local guide, a tall well-spoken and well informed man from Agrigento, and off we are in a mad rush to cover all we can see in a short time. Hera first, Concord still intact and fallen Heracles reinstated partly, vast, impressive though not elegant, not built with marble and not preserved as one is led to believe. Afterwards we thirst less for knowledge than for refreshments that a café stands to readily provide. Goodbye Luigi and the discos of Agrigento.

-

The bus ride to Ragusa is briefly interrupted for a quick espresso at a café on the highway. Everything around here is falling apart and garbage is ever-present, VENDESI plastered on the gates of country homes with neglected gardens and sagging window shutters. Later Gela is weeping thoroughly polluted. That is why when entering the vicinity of Ragusa one is pleasantly surprised to rediscover a world that is orderly, clean and visibly prospering.

Ragusa, hit by a catastrophic earthquake in 1693, was entirely rebuilt and only a few traces of the previous construction exist today. As a result the old city, Ibla, is entirely built in the Baroque style. The new Ragusa is modern and separated from the old one by a wide ravine where the remains of the river run.

The hotel can only be reached on foot; the luggage is shuttled by a small van. With the first contact Ragusa-Ibla enchants the visitor. And although the streets are narrow and curvy, there are plenty of light and flower pots everywhere. On the one end a well maintained park, previously a private garden, is the lungs and window to nature for the inhabitants.

-

Dinner later takes place at Il Barroco Ristorante, just half a block away, where we are joined by Jonathan Bassett and Sonya Conti, owners of the tour company. Well prepared, plentiful and rich multicourse dinner accompanied by local wine closes the evening.

Ragusa 10 May 2010

* 2.38

Today is a day of leisure at Ibla-Ragusa. We get up without alarm clock to savor the breakfast. In spite of an aggravating evening with the business of the Trust we are refreshed.

Local guide is Barbara who takes the group for a historical walk of the old town.

At 15:30 a tour of the Donafugata Palazzo proves to be a disappointment for the place is unmaintained, the gardens reverting to wild anarchy and the exhibits not attractively shown.

Evening on our own finds us in a small family-run restaurant, where one can escape the routine of antipasto, primi and secondi piatti followed by dolci.

Ragusa 11 May 2010

* 2.39

Modica is the next stopover, a city similar but larger than Ragusa with a Baroque heart. Birthplace to Salvatore Quasimodo, it has similarly suffered from the great earthquake as Ragusa; moreover its center received a serious blow by a river flood that crested to over eleven meters in some areas.

Its great cathedral looms over the central square; with its walls built of local cream-color limestone, it is immensely radiant. Across the way lies the old Jewish quarter, whose inhabitants were converted or displaced when the Spanish ruled Sicily.

Modica is known for chocolate manufactured in the traditional Mexican way. A visit to the Bonaiuto chocolate factory gives us the chance to taste and purchase Xócolatl.

-

Noto with a façade reminiscent of Hollywood props feels like a letdown after Modica. Many people fill its streets, students and tourists of all sorts. We agree that the best thing to do is to have a sandwich with a beer and talk at the outdoors table of an espresso bar.

-

Now it has come the time to drive to the celebrated Siracusa on the island of Ortygia. Exhausted, most of us drift to sleep during the bus ride.

Buses are not allowed on the island. A public free shuttle provides transportation from the parking area and over the bridge to the island and to hotel Roma.

Tonight's dinner is organized for the group at an *osteria* in Ortygia but before dinner we pay a visit to Santa Lucia de Sepolto to see a Caravaggio mural. He may have never thought of this area as home but as a temporary asylum from his detractors and he paid for his stay with his labor. The lighting is not bright and the closest distance to the mural is at least 50 meters. I squint trying to observe his bold chiaroscuro without satisfactory results.

Osteria Da Martino serves as host to the tour group tonight. The food is good, usually rich but strangely spicy. A simple dessert is accompanied by sweet wines.

Siracusa 12 May 2010

✤

2.40

The swallows dart in the space above the Piazza del Duomo, free of obligations, of aesthetic comparisons, of historic relativity, of geography, content to preoccupy themselves alone with living, experiencing no joy, sorrow or nostos. To the swallows the Acropolis of Athens or the mines of Syracuse are equivalent, only chosen as their home by a long line of previous generations. What does location mean then for the human traveler who searches for identity?

-

Neapolis was the last of the Siracusan Pentapolis cities that surrounded the port and has a distant view of the seaport. Therein lays the famed Greek Theater that has been partially restored to its former character. Anna Maria, the local guide who seems more Spanish in her gestures and staccato delivery of her oratory, explains the location and function of the theater while below, construction workers assemble props for the upcoming performance of Phaedra. The sea simmers far away under a morning blue sky.

Behind the amphitheater are the stone quarries that were in antiquity places of confinement and heavy labor for convicted criminals, political opponents and ultimately thousands of starving and dying Athenian prisoners. Today a paradise of luxuriant vegetation, they were once hell for those who labored in there.

One wonders if during theater performances the sound of pain and desperation emanating from within Latomie reached the ears of Siracusans.

The Romans after razing Syracuse to the ground modified the theater to suit their needs but ultimately built a closed arena better suited to their games.

I recount the Greek sites we have so far seen and find none to be more inspiring or beautiful or even better preserved (except for the Temple of Concord), than those still standing in Greece. What is unique here is the visible layering of many civilizations on top of each other and the effects of the destructive power of nature. Sicily is a history of ravage upon ravage, human and natural and the persistence of the human element which otherwise is resigned to fate.

The morning tour concludes in the Cathedral, which is a perfect example of a new civilization building on top of the previous civilization layer.

-

Wandering in the small alleys and twisting narrow medieval streets fills one's nostrils with unfamiliar smells together with a suffocating scent of mold. Even though Ortygia is constantly being renovated it remains a very old place that hides its history in the folds of dilapidating walls...

-

Why Calliope? A soft name, the name of a muse, muse of music, euphonic and not aggressive... At the Trattoria Kalliope a small man, the owner of the restaurant, helps with the orders and talks to customers. Outdoors on a small *piazzeta*, tables and chairs make it an inviting corner away from the din of traffic, while Frank Sinatra and Louis Armstrong perform in the mild Syracusan night.

Siracusa 13 May 2010

❊

* 2.41

The last leg of the tour starts this morning with a drive to Piazza Armerina in Southwestern Sicily, which we had left two days ago. The bus enters the Enna region, rich in beauty and agriculture but poor economically. Hills covered with forests, groves of citrus, wheat flow into each other. Now and then, large farmhouses, many in poor repair or abandoned, dot the landscape.

Before visiting the archaeological site we stop for lunch at Trattoria La Ruota, an agro tourism restaurant, less than a mile away from Piazza Armerina. The steep hills surrounding the place are green with the foliage of trees; here and there masses of Scotch broom's yellow bloom add to the golden overtones of sun. At Trattoria La Ruota Luigi joins the group to be once more our local guide.

Piazza Armerina lies at the bottom of a narrow valley surrounded by hills. To get to it one must walk a gauntlet of dozens of tents selling useless souvenirs, post cards, trinkets and food. A long line of tourist buses patiently waits at the parking area.

-

Unflappable Luigi leads the group through an area that is under repair, explaining mysteries with likely and unlikely tales, pointing to details that one would be unlikely to notice, especially with so many people marching through.

We say goodbye to Luigi at Trattoria La Ruota to turn now in a northeastern direction towards the coast and Catagna. The sky is getting darker and is threatening rain. Shortly after Mount Aetna appears in the horizon, raindrops hit the windows. We are in the outskirts of Catagna.

-

Taormina sits on high ground overlooking the Ionian Sea. Like a famous hetaera, she shows off all she has, brazenly. To reach it one must board a small vehicle, thus we, like many other visitors, have to dismount and board shuttle buses. The town is stiflingly packed with people and cars. Every step must be choreographed, every turn of the wheel accurately calculated. The Hotel Villa Belvedere is like a refuge.

-

Dinner reservations at Il Giardino Ristorante for the group have been prearranged by Mariaelena; the dinner lasts for hours, mostly due to kitchen and staff disorganization. Yet it is enjoyable and the service good when not confused. When we walk out it is raining in earnest. A number of us stop at the hotel bar for nightcap.

Taormina 14 May 2010

✤

* *2.42*

The wind furiously whips the vegetation in the garden, bending tree tops and strewing the patio with broken branches, leaves and flowers. The sun shines through fleecy clouds; further in the horizon there are areas of darkness, showers moving quickly across land and sea. The surface of the Ionian Sea is no longer calm; whitecaps are sweeping the great expanse of water.

We explore a bit of the town after breakfast. The Greek Theater is large and decidedly Romanized. As we enter an underground passage, a whirlwind throws sand furiously at us and a passing shower darkens the air. We stay put until the rain abates, then we retreat to the Public Gardens that have the added advantage of being close to the hotel. As the weather improves we move further uptown and try to locate one of the recommended restaurants near the Gate of Messina. Traffic churns throughout the narrow streets and even the pedestrian areas. As we take the road back to the hotel, a small side street trattoria offers the opportunity for a quiet and light lunch.

-

The wind has not stopped; from inside the library of the hotel, in the comfort of closed doors and windows one can look at the distant troubled sea with mild interest. A blond middle aged couple sit facing the sun on armchairs outside, not minding the wind gusts; northerners! Then I resume reading the booklet on Agrigento, skipping little anomalies and ignoring the oddities in the book.

-

We join Garry and Cherry for dinner at an upscale trattoria-pizzeria with wonderful view of the bay. The food is average, the service annoying with too many young waiters who do not have enough to do and trip over each other. Our New Zealanders are cheerful, likeable and much traveled people.

Back in the hotel we think of the excursion to Mount Aetna tomorrow and the forthcoming return home the day after. Our existence here has become fleeting, inconsequential and immaterial.

   Taormina 15 May 2010
✤

* *2.43*

It is the last excursion, a drive to Mount Aetna. In spite of the unstable weather yesterday, the day has begun with clear skies. The wind picks up now and then. Everyone's mind is partially at least drifting to the next stage of their trip, dampening the usual enthusiasm. Mariaelena still cheerful, in spite of a cold she has, counts heads -..., dieciotto. Everyone is present.

-

The winds on Mt Aetna have created problems for the operation of the funicular. We and other visitors pile up in the funicular building waiting for some decision on the means of transportation. Finally large truck buses, not unlike the Movitruck of Salta in Argentina, are called to service.

The bleak landscape whipped by wind becomes bleaker and more alien as the vehicle moves higher and higher. One can see the snow-covered peak surrounded by white clouds approaching. Below the valley is disappearing in the haze of moisture and fine volcanic ash. Here and there is a little sign of life, a small tuft of grass clinging in a crevice of the lava, which often is draped in ice crystals. The vehicles stop at the last refuge before the final push to the top.

Some of the group has elected to take a different vehicle to the closest point to the caldera. The rest take a hike in the thin freezing wind and black lava earth. Later on everyone gathers in the warmth of the refuge to watch a video on Mt Aetna and to try the Foco di Aetna, a liqueur specialty of the area. The results of tasting the liqueur are hilarious and a photo opportunity.

Because the winds have abated, the funicular returns to service giving us the chance to view different aspects of the mountainsides. At the bottom there are a number of lodges with refreshments and food.

We return to the hotel to begin packing our luggage. Most of us will rise very early tomorrow morning to leave for Catagna with the bus of the tour and our faithful driver Vincenzo.

-

The farewell dinner at A Zamarra begins early with toasts, photos and recognition of the services of the tour leader and the bus driver. Both are going tomorrow to different cities, different parts and different schedules which their working program calls for. And the group equally will split in different directions, even though most of our companions will be flying to the States. We eat and drink, thinking back on the days spent together and not much paying attention to the meal. I make small talk with Vincenzo, a nice and hard-working person. We are worlds apart and then maybe we are very close.

I set the alarm for 3:00 am.

> Taormina 16 May 2010
> ✻

* 2.44

Vincenzo is waiting for us on the bus at the parking lot; he has already loaded the luggage. Mariaelena verifies that everyone who should be is aboard and remains behind to take care of the rest of the group. It is dark, just a hint of light begins to show on the horizon to the east. The bus heads south on the highway among cars and trucks. Then dawn manifests with a hint of color reflected upon the snow of Mt Aetna's peak to the west.

We arrive at the Catagna airport in good time. We say farewell to Vincenzo who will drive back to Palermo. With luggage in tow we enter a modern airport to begin the long voyage back home.

> Flying 17 May 2010
> ✻

* 2.45

The expanse of water in the late afternoon, while one stands on the little bridge of Capitola, simmers in blue and azure. Far away the land protuberance cradles the city of Monterrey just barely visible. Sunlight filters dark shadows and off-shore winds have driven the fog bank miles out in the Pacific Ocean. At the little estuary ducks dive and children play on the sand. The face of the golden land returns with the early summer.

Daniel has grown into a young man now with sense of responsibility. His face has taken a darker look beyond that of the stubble growing. Tomorrow in cap and gown he will enter the adult world of struggle.

Santa Cruz June 13 2010

* 2.46

Summer solstice, hazy skies greet the painful and slow awakening from sleepless night. A strange weekend, yet with another marker, the passing of the last survivor of my mother's generation. A disembodied voice in the phone, a message left from this friend, grief and relief at the same time. In childhood we stood together in the emptying school yard plotting the route home. What did we talk about, no recollection left, perhaps avoiding extra work or thinking of history. Yet I still see him and my mother looking at us with inquisitive eye and hear protective voices as they were, fixed in time. Now one more shadow populates the invisible world that haunts us with omissions.

Fiddletown 21 June 2010

* 2.47

Saturated by color light fills summer air layered foliage tree shadows recline to west earth with still fresh feel eye aches from brilliance and heart with yearning would it that be a time of youthful wonder

Fiddletown 30 June 2010

❦

* 2.48

He remembered as if he were looking at the face, so alive still with the questioning look and the black moustache, the face he knew as a boy looks him in the eye with a slight smirk. He remembers his name without trouble as if it were then, in the days he frequented the patisserie with classmates. - A profiterole, Laki, they would say, or a mille-feuille, or a coffee. A friend he was of sorts to a new generation that is passing through with high aspirations and ready to move on and away. As he thinks of him, he realizes he was only a few years older, a significant difference in a time of war and turbulence. – Laki, a brandy, no better make it two, and come sit down with us to talk about the life that did not happen.

   Fiddletown 8 July 2010

❧

* *2.49*

Necessity or precaution dictates putting out drip lines to new vines thus determining today's work. Summer is now certain and part of daily experience and since the sun remains close to its highest trajectory one can dream of cold and wet weather vicariously. The rest of the world now and then intrudes in the solitude of the farm...

   Fiddletown 21 July 2010

❧

* *2.50*

A clove of garlic and a green grape berry first thing in the morning; that marked the start of the month of August. The grapes are green, small and hidden behind leaves, the weather pleasantly hot and the sky deep blue. No one woke me up yesterday morning with the ritual food in hand, the birds kept on singing while next door a tractor quietly growled amidst vineyards. Thus August made his entrance again.

   Fiddletown 2 August 2010

* *2.51*

The impact symbols have in our perception of the world is significant but non-quantifiable. How could there be taxonomy of symbols when their content is not fixed but variable according to circumstantial environment. Even if one were to accept the idea of universal symbols a case could be made for their shifting contents with time and place.

    Fiddletown 10 August 2010

* 2.52

Snail tracks, the passage of time has left behind, vague memories waiting the first autumn rains... Every morning the sun rises later, its rectangular seal of light moves steadily now toward the north wall.

At night dreams take shape of warm familiar body which remains mysterious and alien under the dim light of introspection. Where are now those sun-dappled life-filled summer days from the strangely sequestered space of the past?

    Fiddletown 23 August 2010

* 2.53

Time we don't understand because we refuse to accept the immutability it contains. It is perceived by comparing different instances of memory; it is the delta of A' to A'+1 but since it is impossible to reverse the order of memory or more accurately revert to a previous state of being we are frustrated. Time becomes a limiting obsession with unidirectional dimensionality that complicates our understanding of the external world; it would have been perhaps better if its conception had never existed.

    Fiddletown 25 August 2010

* 2.54

The state in this world is becoming more unstable than usual, resources are being exhausted, population is increasing exponentially, nations are mismanaged, individuals succumb to greed, internal discipline is absent and the climate is undergoing a global change. Even more disturbing is the trend towards religious zealotry in the Christian and Muslim camps, which rejects reasoning and logical thinking. What does the future hold for humanity?

    Fiddletown 26 August 2010

* 2.55

At the opposite side of the Earth the Sun follows the same path as it moves to southern territory while I hold on to a memory desperately fearful it will be replaced by the void of absence. Of the past presences of life companions during different phases of my story I know not exactly how many have vanished.

 I met Vasilis Papatzanis fifty years ago while I was applying for a foreign student exchange position with AIESEC; as past president of the organization he had insights I did not and he did not hesitate to give me valuable advice. We became friends over time, we saw each other infrequently though that did not diminish a friendship that spanned time and space. We shared fellowship and travel during our recent visits to Greece rediscovering his impish sense of humor and Katerina's radiant smile.

 As the day wears on, filling memory gaps with bits and pieces not belonging, I refuse to let go of a certainty of existence, the twinkle in his eye and the peal of laughter still so resonant.

 (Vasilis perished on 31 July in Athens after more than two years of battling leukemia).

    Fiddletown 10 September 2010

* 2.56

Troubled night tosses fragments from the fabric of time to the wind images formed or dissolved in some mysterious non-sequential process the observer observed the observation dissected the shards stored for an imposing mosaic yet to be composed by order of preference sounds of owl and other nocturnal birds inhibit such attention as chance brings this way the moving air of a troubled night without moon...

   Fiddletown 13 September 2010

* 2.57

Tenuous connections of the information highway filaments dangling in the wind lives break apart so fragile themselves those relationships of unadvised need thrown away with broken furniture heaps of discarded memory serving only to sharpen the pain and misery.
 We don't know what all this will result in though it is almost certain it will be the breakup of the marriage with unknown fallout. This year has brought a lot of tumult and grief...

   Fiddletown 15 September 2010

* 2.58

I see you also have become preoccupied with time, which has to run its course, damn us all. Without it we would not have departures or arrivals, separations or reunions; without it we would not know wither we sail and miss no one but time itself. Time is the fabric we are made of and not an external dimension we can measure accurately; when we are gone so is time, it exists no more.

   Fiddletown 21 September 2010

* 2.59

See how the weather has changed, a small pepper grows fiery red, birds fly south coming or leaving, you and I stay in a world that turns sober and cold.

The rain is expected but has not yet arrived. Next to a strip of green land lies the ocean constantly lashing at the coast. And here is like a refuge from time only it feels false in the outskirts of a self-important city.

    Half Moon Bay 23 October 2010

* 2.60

Windy and wintry, rain splashes on the pavement or threads the pine needles of swaying trees. Mood swings from one pole to the other, fails the vision in detail and recoils to the depths of dream. Inside comfort pushes back rigor of outdoor necessity. Here longing for a mythical dimension time reshapes itself in simile without destination...

    Half Moon Bay 24 October 2010

* 2.61

Pasadena and S. California which were home once have been released from their bonds; instead I see another city and another metropolis with vague ties from the past.

The wind kept the transparency of light as it whipped palm fronds savagely; we drove steadily through heavy traffic thinking of all the changes that happened and all that are in the future. The farm is left behind for a week's rest after the harvest.

With Arturo and Domna we spend the first evening at their place and out dining at Malbec. Surprisingly fatigue has not been a problem. Friends are catalysts of information that may or may not be substantive.

Star Trek is still showing on television but the newscasters are now unfamiliar faces. Many things have changed; an air of certain shabbiness is pervasive.

Pasadena 09 November 2010

*2.62

The power of adapting quickly changes perceptions; what was yesterday unusual, unfamiliar today escapes observation. The sun keeps shining on Los Angeles and on the transverse mountain range to the north.

Life is coming back to the battered economy; you can see it in the increasing numbers of people who spend for entertainment. Still the streets are not filled with crowds, at least not at the beginning of the week.

John reminisces on the ARCO years, time that has left scars along with good memories. Corfu is packed with people; we sit outside enjoying good weather and clean air. The unremarkable food lingers on the plate.

The streets in Old Pasadena are quiet in the cool evening. The Afghani restaurant seems like a lighthouse in the city night scene. Last year we had to change last minute plans because the place was packed; tonight only a few tables are filled giving us the quiet we longed for to talk with Erika. The conversation unfolds like a gentle mist in night darkness with a bottle of wine and food that exhibits Hindu-Iranian influences. We linger with Erika past the restaurant's closing time. Outside Old Pasadena shows off more new buildings and many stalled construction projects. Erika suffers from back pain and she looks fragile.

Pasadena 10 November 2010

*2.63

From the window the yellow-gray layer smears the southern horizon; the Santana wind is over letting the smog stream inland. It will be warmer today.

For two days we had a taste of Southland's freeway and street driving as we drove to Santa Monica and Glendale. Many an inexperienced or inattentive driver creates unsafe conditions on the roads that often combined with high traffic volumes result in gridlock. After a decade of living away surprisingly I have not lost the instinctive familiarity with the road grid.

West Los Angeles has become more densely populated, feeling as if neighbors practically breathe down each other's neck. Finding parking in Santa Monica is an exercise in frustration that we avoid because we can park in the parking area of the two buildings we visit, the largest one vacant for nearly a year shows all the maintenance neglect that USPS demonstrated. We take measurements, discuss options, and discover details, all the things needed to come up with plans for attracting an occupant.

After lunch in a bakery at 17th and Montana Streets we visit the smaller building, whose leaseholder is having problems meeting rent payments. The interior of the building shows no signs of neglect, thankfully there are customers coming in, hopeful signs. The story we get is the same as last year, which we know it to be for the most part truthful. Business is in a slump, it can be seen in the number of FOR LEASE signs posted throughout the city.

......

At Gus and Maria's place Bogie slumbers wrapped in a blanket, deaf and blind in his old age. A mirror of human fate the little dog suffers his destiny with dignity.

The light rail shuttles us to S. Pasadena for dinner at the Bistro de la Gare, a familiar by now restaurant. Gus and Maria look both good even though she seems to be a trifle depressed.

The evening concludes at their place where we chat around the little kitchen table.

.....

Next morning after breakfast at Whole Foods we go shopping for shoes at Pasadena's Macy's, but not finding what I am after, we commit to going to Glendale Galleria after our lunch at Malbec with Vicente and Maria Luisa. A refreshing lunch is followed by driving through a traffic snarl and shopping in a crowded

Glendale mall that ultimately yields a pair of shoes and a special lotion for Elaine.

…..

In the evening we make the best with victuals and wine from Whole Foods in our motel room.

Pasadena 12 November 2010

* 2.64

The little dog is underfoot; the little dog is Thumper and wants to play. We arrived one hour early, then realizing our mistake we retreated for an hour to our motel. Daniel and his girlfriend Nikki have also arrived in a red Mustang. Nilda cooks while Dan serves wine. The large oven is out of commission from a defective control board, consequently Dan cannot prepare his specialty, pizza. The simple 1940s gas stove we had for years in S. California never gave us trouble.

Daniel is growing into an adult in spite of his looks; in a few years he may have his own family. For the time being he survives the bad economic times.

Dan recalls his student years and the beginning of our friendship. It is an odd sensation sitting and listening about the past delivered in such a matter of fact way even though inwardly he is probably nostalgic and emotional.

…..

Lunch with Gail at a Thai restaurant in Pasadena is pleasant and animated without awkward moments as in the past. She has transcended her insecurity. There are some things we can be grateful for in old age.

The sun shines over S. California, the blue skies shimmer in a Santana breeze; here and there some the foliage reminds you of the season, otherwise it is summer forever...

Pasadena 13 November 2010

�֍

* 2.65

No one calls the phone that sits on the table in the living room; the land- line connected telephone has become a fixture without use in a matter of a few years. In the beginning of the decade when we were here visiting it served as the main means of communication. Our friends called us at the hotel to get in touch and we used the phone to transact business even to get e-mail. Wire, the king, was so suddenly supplanted by wireless communications, a familiar story of so many things, business, professions and trades in these times of rapid change. Changes, changes for us and our personal world, changes for all, the impact of which can be seen and felt but not truly measured.

The traffic yesterday Saturday evening at 6:00 pm was chocking. Standstill on every freeway we drove by, panic crept in the closed automobile cabin. NO EXIT. Never before have we had a similar experience. Rivers of thousands of car lights hardly moving on the road grid that crisscrosses rolling hills.

Exhausted we arrive at Susi's house, a refuge from the nightmare. Even though it feels like a time from past it is not immune to the harshness of tonight. I measure changes within and without. At the table and in the living room everything registers normal but when the slideshow starts again I am stunned. The evening is too short to communicate the feelings within; all too soon we find ourselves on the road again returning to Pasadena. At one o'clock in the morning it is possible to imagine again the freeways as they were twenty or so years ago.

.....

The same noon we gather broken pieces of another life under blue skies in the Plaza Las Fuentes. At the California Pizza Kitchen we sip wine, savor food and talk about picking up the pieces with Mei and Julie. Probably everyone wonders what the future will bring and where Larry is now.

We make a last venture to meet some of our friends in Claremont and Pasadena. Quieter day and very beautiful as can be the rare times one sees in Southern California. Hal and Lil are

settling in for their later years, the disappointments having taken their toll yet they are more at peace than I would have thought.
....

Later in the evening even Rodanthi does not complain too much, seemingly being immersed in her home and the memories that live therein.
…...

In the morning again we retrieve our presents and personal articles as we prepare to return home.

Pasadena 15 November 2010

* 2.66

The changes of weather are distinct and sudden; from this autumnal color celebration nature will recede to the colorless monotony of winter. Whereas the earth becomes the target of the eye throughout spring, summer and autumn, winter shifts the focus to the sky with its changing moods. But none is sweeter to the eye than sunlight when it breaks out of the lead-gray clouds.

The trip to S. California was tiring. Finally on the third day back I feel integrated to the environment; time to gather fruit, another bucket of Chandler walnuts, sort the pears and apples in the basement. Although rain is coming only a limited amount of walnuts will find their way to the drying frame. We are bound by our ability to move the product in the market.

The truck is in for its annual maintenance, a major one (repeated) to keep it running smoothly. Finally I have had enough of the other automotive service I patronized for the last ten years; I try the local shop and have lunch at the Vintage Market.

Plymouth 17 November 2010

*2.67

Christmas Day that does not summon Christmas Past when the first light of dawn seeps in the bedroom. Ghosts of Christmas Past have receded in dark corners of the mind gnawing at the root of the Tree of Life, hideous trolls that materialize this festive season. Festive it was once when one contemplated the future with expectations of near certainty, not now when companions of many decades perish at each turn of a tortuous road.

Walking out on the veranda I am struck by the light emanating from the East. The sun rises above the mountains sheathed in clouds. The peaceful land engulfs me with lack of expectations, filling me with animist submission to the fate of all living things. Once upon a time there was Christmas...

Fiddletown 25 December 2010

*2.68

At five o'clock in the morning everything is frozen outside, a thin sheet of ice extends on the carport floor having captivated? inside it a moment of summer. In a state between sleep and awareness the mind trapped can for eternity spin examining the same thought or series of thoughts. The only exit from the impasse is through sleep that ultimately lulls the mind transporting it to a surreal and fantastic realm.

Later the cold intensifies before sunrise; the senses return to a resting body...

Fiddletown 30 December 2010

*2.69

In the afternoon blue sky and bright sunlight change the landscape. While fog was here everything seemed subdued and melancholic unable to alter the mood that lingered overnight and found refuge in the songs from the album played. The melancholy of Greece rises in the music and verses that gently shift through the remains of hope. Life is brief, sad and unpredictable; life is all man has to lose in his passage through this world. On the wall the frame with photos from school years fill my heart with pity; those faces which will never leave me are a piece of personal history, a cry of despair for lost hopes and aspirations. I have lost count of the many individuals who may have departed for ever.

 Fiddletown 17 January 2011

* *2.70*

I looked forward for so long to servicing the HONDA Civic; I had almost forgotten the beautiful views from the Shingle Springs heights. In early afternoon on a mild sunny day, one can see clearly the snow that gleams on the Sierra ridges; it can be touched, almost. Your musings soft like the breeze take away worries of financial, legal and existential substance. The car hoisted up the rack is taken care for a few more thousand miles...

 Shingle Springs 27 January 2011

* *2.71*

For Gus:

>Love, the charioteer who raises
>the tender four, her life bound
>to theirs in unending labor through
>the passage of all time

In the passage of time but a few fleeting instances now vanished in all the nights of turbulence or in the days of labor what matters then this effort of naught that appeared by means of a strange land while at rest and while overlooking all the battles with windmills

    Fair Oaks 25 February 2011

* 2.72

March breezes weave through naked branches of dormant trees awakening springtime blooms. The almonds have responded almost as soon as the flowering quince has begun to display coral color in a colorless landscape. Every morning resurrection becomes more visible filling with emotion the recurring lost memories of time ago; in their shadow wander faces not of this earth as they were and as they will continue to be as long as the bearer is here, casting melancholy on the festival of life.

    Fiddletown 8 March 2011

* 2.73

Begin at the beginning laying out a grid of paths not taken; what are left a lifetime and the least significant trails...
    I weave whispers in the warp of dawn; I pull apart all patterns leaving behind the fracas of a mockingbird. Here to the despair of mountain ridges quietly flows the stream...

    Fiddletown 16 March 2011

* 2.74

Springtime brings back visible life to the bare framework of trees; the branches burst out with flowers and young leaves.

It is a time of exhilaration and pain like that of human birth. Blooming trees undergo uncertain weather changes, from sunny and mild to cold, rainy and even snowy. No one can predict what the outcome will be, the damage sustained or the crop to be borne. Spring is a cruel and unpredictable season that often drives me to lowest moods or the highest exultations.

Fiddletown 17 March 2011

❦

* 2.75

The dam breached lets out a flood of images, thoughts and interconnections that become bridges to deeply buried memories. Now and then faces emerge from non-existence calling their dues with somber voices. The opportunities abound for new discoveries of ancient explorations; Easter is near to the heart of springtime resurrection celebrated by the bloom of the apple trees.

Fiddletown 19 April 2011

❦

* 2.76

Timeless Pasadena on the foot of San Gabriel Mountains extends its fair weather delighting all travelers who come her way. In springtime green and fresh from rains that reached this part of the S. California desert hosts the foothill mockingbird that serenades unto dawn the moon sailing a starry sky.

Now it seems eons since we lived here, before the move to the foothills of Sierra Nevada; even then population, traffic and redevelopment were on the increase. One adjusts to changes, ignoring good or bad side except for those that age itself brings; the validity of observations then becomes suspect.

Emily guided us past a traffic alert at Lincoln Ave. as we joined a stream of cars rerouted through New York Drive. Everything looks almost unchanged, the houses, the gardens, the trees and the mountains... except for rows of new houses high up on the side of the mountain, proudly surveying the area that has burned several times in recent memory. The phone begins to ring, solitude is over; friends have discovered us fresh from the day-long drive on Highway US 99.

....

At the Pasadena Royale we are given a suite that is laid out as mirror image to all we previously had; the feeling is strange, almost as if your life is reversed.

....

Francisco looks old, he has reached the age men become grandfathers only he is still a recent father to this impish and coy young girl. Even Rosie looks more mature gaining in confidence and bone weight. They have gone through hard times and more are ahead; I try not to think about it, I despair of the possibilities available. The waiter at Fu Shing is pleasant to all and very fatherly to Daniela, he likes children, perhaps not having any of his own. The little girl walks out loaded with gifts, from us a dress and from the waiter a bag of fortune cookies. Francisco insists we visit them on our way to Henderson, a detour for us. We leave things at that as we board the car. We are back at the motel in a few minutes...

Pasadena 28 April 2011

* *2.77*

After a restless night sleep the mountains, so visibly present in Pasadena, at sunrise are cloaked in white gauzy clouds. Mornings set in motion memory, action plans and yearnings for material and immaterial things. The city is already awake, the streets full of traffic as the sun penetrates the morning haze.

At Whole Foods the breakfast is simple, rolls and latte, the conversation hushed and pensive. We linger as time permits before setting out to find such items as we need.

Colorado Boulevard is still familiar with its kind of pedestrians and the rushing traffic and despite many improvements or restorations; its buildings quickly take on a shabby look.

Lunch at the Delhi Palace is a modest buffet, though the pleasure is seeing Rodanthi who looks quite well after her latest health threat. I taste okra spears without spice I would have wished, potatoes that are wilted like us after so many years of life.

....

With the car in the TARGET parking structure we visit the Pacific Asia Museum, its exhibits more familiar since our trip to India and Bhutan. Slowly we wander through rooms of exhibits, musing on the meaning and content of culture. In the courtyard the garden is illuminated by the Pacific sun of this island of California.

....

More surprises during the walk westward on Colorado Boulevard; stores that have closed, others have opened, vacancies, but worst of all, Il Fornaio has emptied out the always welcoming espresso bar that was in the side of the building. To rest briefly we stop at Europane, a poor substitute for Il Fornaio.

....

Dan and Nilda are talking to the host of Celestino, a still popular and busy restaurant for two decades in Pasadena. At the table over wine and food, we talk and observe the hurried to and fro of the waiters. Every time in Pasadena I am addressed as Dottore, it seems, something having to do with Caltech being an integral part of the community and my appearance.

We all laugh a great deal recalling Nilda's eccentric behavior during our trip to France. Of course given the same circumstances she would act the same way again.

Pasta con le sarde is prepared the same way as presently Sicilian restaurants do, that is, with mashed sardines instead of grilled whole ones. Their preparation does not have the abundant ricotta Sicilians use and the aromatics. The service is more rushed tonight but still attentive without being intrusive.

We bid goodbye to our friends in a mild spring night of Southern California.

    Pasadena 29 April 2011

❋

* 2.78

The Southland is about to warm up, familiar face for many years as it switched seasons unpredictably. I have become aware though of one aspect that I had totally forgotten, the hazy mornings, marine influence which later in a hot day is transformed into smog.

．．．．．．．

The visit to our former neighbors brings us back to the cul-de-sac that was the immediate surroundings for three decades. Our former house has not appreciably changed other than a coat of paint and a low wall surrounding the patio. The redwoods thrive and the hedge that was our privacy all those years has attained new heights. A toilette fixture leans against the back fence, objects dismantled bit by bit that have been an invisible part of the lives of others.

I suffer Andy's prattle quietly; he has not changed, I just have forgotten how annoying he can be after a while. Stories about cruises, the kids, the neighbors and eventually about a former friend we had met. His projects are the same and long-term since some remain permanently unfinished.

The restaurant at La Cañada we go with, Dish, has replaced Reflections without improving it. This has been one of the most poorly made tuna sandwiches I have had in years.

．．．．．．．

We take a stroll at S. Lake Avenue before our evening get-together. Several storefronts are empty, shops we knew are gone; the most prevalent type of the new breed of shops caters to young well-heeled parents. On San Pasqual the sign of times: one remaining old Pasadena home, boarded and fenced is waiting for a housing developer and across the street the self-proclaimed top luxury condominium of the city, barely finished, sparsely occupied, is undergoing repairs. The old trees on the street serenely look on.

......

Our friends further south on S. Lake Avenue are at it again with house improvements. The house and garden are immaculate as always and the three little dogs noisy and curious; I miss Oliver the master cat.

After a glass of wine, business talk and personal exchanges, we drive to a South Pasadena restaurant that appears to be quite popular. Although we enjoy the outdoors ambience, the food is unremarkable in all aspects but its price. I begin to wonder if Los Angeles has begun to decline as a culinary center or if in general restaurants have been changing to accommodate different tastes of the public.

Pasadena 30 April 2011

2.79

After a cool night the sunny morning presages a warm if not hot day. Opening eyes is like pulling down the stores on the dream windows and locking the darkness within.

At Whole Foods a wholesome breakfast with Muesli rolls and latte further restores confidence in the day ahead.

Promenading on the Caltech grounds is peaceful beyond imagination; springtime blooms and new foliage transform angular architecture to playful deceiving curvatures; the two ponds where koi used to swim are now clogged with lotus that has begun to bloom. In the far corner of the campus, at the end of the Olive Walk the tables of the Athenaeum stand ready for lunch covered with starched white tablecloths. By the Library the Engelmann Oak comes back to life overcoming its diminished stature. All the vitality of the moment finds a restful point in the walkway with the splashing waters where tall pine trees hide a singing mockingbird and cast their shadow on graceful benches.

....

The merging of the 134 and the 101 freeways is an exercise in madness Southland style, one that often comes to a standstill because of heavy traffic. This afternoon the cars speed forward unimpeded passing familiar on-ramps. Almost four decades ago we often took the Forest Lawn Drive exit to Barham Boulevard on the way to visiting the Potts. The shape of the land has changed over the years, the familiar signs submerged in the new reality.

At Bel Air also many changes are evident, the Skirball Museum has expanded, the 405 freeway is under expansion and many new houses have been added to the exclusive development our friends live. Even after eight years of absence the familiar environment cloaks changes time has brought about. Talking in the kitchen is easy, casual and like times before; with the lamb in the oven everyone moves outdoors for conversation, wine and appetizers. Michael and his friend Evan show up later when the table is set for early dinner. Jo has drunk too much scotch, Herb is relaxed and we all get to discussing politics and economics. Cessi makes our dinner easy by working hard in the kitchen. We depart early for Pasadena.

....

A phone call from Erika, she cancels our get together tomorrow evening; her pneumonia is not under control. Then the news broadcast on all TV channels of Obama's sudden nation address to announce the death of Osama bin Laden by Special Forces in Pakistan; he escaped his capture by getting shot.

Pasadena 1 May 2011

* 2.80

Another beautifully clear and hot day dawns over S. California. It is the day to drive to Santa Monica though little we know how bad the traffic we encounter will be.

After an interminable stop and go drive we arrive at the destination with only a few minute delay.

Santa Monica is packed with cars, its streets, parking lots and parking places. I cannot imagine living under such conditions, yet once we would have been very happy to have settled down here by the Santa Monica bluffs.

Any illusions about Sunset Blvd. have are shattered by the return drive that begins at PCH and Sunset Blvd. junction. Other than the most affluent segments the remaining portions are shabby as ever. Wilshire would have been a quicker way to return to Pasadena.

....

Fu Shing is quiet on Monday evening, a respite from a hectic day; the food is satisfying and the conversation sparse. We consider tomorrow's departure as another mark in the map of our lives; we think of friends and weep a little.

Pasadena 2 May 2011

* 2.81

The gray changes barely to dusty rose when I rise for our departure to Henderson, Nevada. From the window one can gaze out over roofs of houses and small apartment buildings to the south; the outlines are softened by the morning haze which will soon dissolve to make room for another clear and hot day.

....

Long and tedious is the drive through high desert to Las Vegas with a short stop to the Mad Greek; the restaurant run by Mexicans has little connection to Greece except for many posters and a curious sign above the door visible at exit time, ΨΕΥΤΟΤΑΒΕΡΝΑ. It is a humorous and at the same time sarcastic explanation of what this restaurant is.

After checking in at the Comfort Inn at Henderson and a brief rest we drive to the house of the friends we are here to visit, located in the outer rim of a gated community and a few miles from the hotel.

We find both of them looking well, in spite of Donna's recent health problem. They eagerly show their house before sitting at the garden for a bite and a glass of wine. There Harry goes on in great detail over his involvement with the Club of the Community. He has few listening skills and thus it becomes a long tedious self-centered monologue. Finally we drive to the Club for supper where we conclude the evening. Afterwards we drive out to the hotel under GPS directions. The entire basin is bathed in light.

Henderson, NV 3 May 2011

2.82

Starting from Las Vegas to Death Valley we cross high desert comprising valleys and low mountains of the Amargosa Range bearing unmistakable signs of past volcanic activity; scrub and tufts of grass dot the otherwise bare land and the distant mountain ranges wear soft lavender gray colors in the bright morning sunlight. In higher regions there is a clear similarity to Andean Puna while multi-colored hillsides remind one of the Northwest Argentinan landscape. Soon after crossing the border between Nevada and California we enter the Death Valley National Park. At the entry an automated ticket kiosk is not functioning, frustrating visitors willing to pay for entrance.

The most spectacular part of Death Valley is located in the Southeast part, close to the US190 highway entrance, Zabriski Point. From a high point we can survey the surrounding area of badlands of fantastic shapes and colors while in the distant horizon we see the snow-capped peaks of Mt Whitney. There is no plant life in the immediate vicinity; the toxicity of the minerals is lethal. The heat is rising quickly as the day progresses and we resume our driving. Further on we find the renowned Furnace Creek Inn, which already has moved into its off-season period and the Park Visitors' Center that outfits us with a map of the park.

On the road again we reach one of the lowest points in North America before beginning a long ascent to Panamint Range, then again we descend to Panamint Valley to cross a mountain range again to enter the Owens Valley as we head to Lone Pine.

....
After a refreshing cup of ice cream we opt to drive through the Alabama Hills to Mt Whitney Portal where snow still lies on the side of the road and cold clear water cascades filling the stream, irrigating Lone Pine. It is a refreshing moment of solitude and contrasts with the mood of the rest of the day.

Lone Pine 4 May 2011

*2.83

The morning of departure from Ashland, sunshine draped over the hills holding the darkness of clouds at bay. Disappointment prevails in my thoughts about this trip; the weather has been miserable and the recasting of classical plays by Shakespeare and Molière low-brow travesty. We have now become very hesitant to repeat this trip for theatrical reasons. We hope Sissy has enjoyed the change of scenery in spite of the poor performances.

Greece meanwhile is mauled by its EU partners; what has happened to the visionary spirit that conjured the European Common Market?

Ashland, OR 27 May 2011

*2.84

The noise level is deafening in the small place packed with people. Shingle Springs Coffee Company is doing well after a two year business downturn. It is a small consolation in the present economic woes. Shut our ears to the dire predictions and hope for a better future in which everyone learns to be a responsible citizen and the politicians learn to rely on cogent economists for financial guidance.

......

Sissy has returned to her world, family, problems and duties; perhaps something from our short encounter has left an impression which might help her cope better and boost her critical thinking. Meanwhile I have come to realize how difficult is for me to share my sense and sensibility with even dear friends. A lifetime together has made that possible with Elaine; I am gratified and grateful. Of my friends in Greece who would be the one that I could best share my deepest feelings and doubts?

......

Days of rain have given way to blue skies and sun, at least up to this point. The mountain outline is already covered with clouds, temperature has stalled in the 60s and my outlook has darkened; I long for summer...

Shingle Springs 7 June 2011

2.85

Other paths through dreams that lead to the other side that exists in the night unfulfilled wishes or alternate memories represent the whole never assembled with insufficient recollection that which is sequestered in another point of time which we know not how to reach at will... and the faces of people we crossed paths with those we loved or hated those that left us carrying the burden of yearning *saudade* or remorse spring up from flattened aged film reels like fading or unpredictable movies without plot the nights which carry the seed of impending dawn...

Without warning July is here having reset the yearly rain accumulation; we start our life anew when sheets of heat descend to smother earth during the longest days of the year. Time to turn inward for relief from memories of earlier summers at the blue sea with seahorses and marine nymphs...

Fiddletown 2 July 2011

* *2.86*

We should consider direction a relative measure and in case of time irrelevant or deceiving; how relevant is it to say "come down to see us" to someone living in a different location when there are no clear conventions on the use of up or down in geography? If not stricken out the relative reference is mostly ignored by the listeners or interpreted according to their own point of reference.

Fiddletown 25 July 2011

* *2.87*

The past is present the dreams are past the pain of living covers the hours with oblivion little by little inducing a state of non-existence which vision refutes with images of another season thus rendering it impossible to extricate from self-awareness

Three months have passed, time of intense activity in the farm and not a line of writing to eliminate foibles from the mind. The summer is gone before it started cool weather for the most part that deprives the sense of the season and leaves fruit hanging unripe on tree and vine. Only people who vanish regularly in the darkness of memory keep the clock ticking mercilessly.

Fiddletown 18 October 2011

West to East

* 2.88

The human frailty is the net of time that sums up his existence irrevocably extracting and accumulating sequentially snapshots of information. Trapped in a world of precedence his existence becomes confined to the terror of anticipation. In a different universe perhaps the order of things is utterly alien with life unbounded by beginning and end, where sequence is unknown and history a concept that cannot exist.

...
In Southland nothing quite falls in place as it once did; change has hollowed out content leaving façades behind like Sirens calling the returning Odysseus. Disappointment hides behind images eliciting the past as it was once or as it is thought to have been.

Long is the drive and arduous between farm and megalopolis, hours of moving through space with little physical motion of limbs. Changes subtly register to the eye and brain to prompt a discussion or argument about such and such landscape feature having been part of it previously.

...
In the evening Mexican food proves a poor choice but perhaps no poorer than any other kind of cuisine in a world of mass produced fast food.

Pasadena 8 November 2011

* 2.89

Bright sunlight blazes, clear blue sky frames the mountains to the north and the tall palms sway in the slight breeze. This is wintertime in fairyland.

Over a cup of latte we plan the first day in Pasadena which is no longer home but a familiar place that is undergoing transformations with the passage of time.

The replacement non-prescription glasses serve their purpose very well, I can read. This is the second time I find myself without glasses because of a mishap although because my familiarity with the area the event is less traumatic in finding replacement.

At the Fu Shing restaurant the menu is versatile and diverse and pleases the tastes of all in the company. Gail Reynolds Natzler, for 44 years friend since the Santa Monica period, celebrates our presence here and our upcoming birthdays. The narrow booth table at the end of the dining room gives Elaine a place to rest her injured leg. This is time for thanksgiving; we share thoughts and memories, we share a quiet time as if at the end of the world.

...
Dan and Nilda pull up in the parking lot of the Pasadena Royale as we are ready to enter the hotel lobby; six months is a long time in between seeing friends. They look unchanged and in good health; the car is the same and running strong as we enter the freeway. The madness of traffic congestion is unabated even at 8:00 pm; when you look beyond the wall of cars the lights of the metropolis paint a magical landscape.

Another successful Drago brothers' restaurant, La Panzanella in Sherman Oaks, hides in a narrow alley. The reception is typical Drago, formal friendly and refined; the noisy dining room is packed with people. From now to the end of the evening conversation becomes very difficult. The menu is interesting but not as eclectic as Celestino's and the food itself lacks the distinction of its Pasadena sibling.

We return to the hotel room by 11:00 pm ready to rest after the first full day here in Southland.

Pasadena 9 November 2011

* *2.90*

Pilgrimage through the heart of Los Angeles where yet another skyscraper puffs out one of its glass sides in the direction of the ocean, blue wedge uncomfortably perched above the twisted corridor of vehicles. The heart of the metropolis pulses with steel blood that surges through narrow arteries bound for all directions. Familiar route, different vehicles, other people but I have the same sensation on the way to Santa Monica.

The westernmost side of the basin bulges with construction exploiting every bit of available space creating an asphyxiating sensation to the motorists of the inadequate street grid inherited from another era.

Fortunately there are some empty parking spaces at the Trust property where I can pull in. The business part of the visit takes over an hour but we find it rewarding that the building has been restored to good condition by viable tenants; the process of transition has taken almost two years and it was filled with uncertainty and aggravation.

The pilgrimage to a time past is completed by the reverse travel to spacious and eye-pleasing Pasadena. At California Pizza Kitchen seated in a booth by a window, images from two decades ago recapture friends, some for ever gone. One cannot but be conscious of the depreciating quality of life, food in the restaurants, quality of merchandise, increasing prices, congestion and unrest.

...

Hugo's is a mini restaurant with maxi prices, loud dining room and sub-par menu. We are here to see a friend and that makes the Sierra Madre restaurant company perfect. Erika, Elaine's close friend of many years arrives a little late because of the predictably unpredictable traffic snarl on the freeway across Pasadena. Another year has elapsed since our last meeting, more frailties have crept in. Wine and food fuel the conversation until we are nearly forcibly evicted from the closing restaurant. – It's closing so early like Amador County, comments Elaine. ...

Pasadena 10 November 2011

2.91

As yesterday today is again an overcast day though mild; the mountains have stepped back to distance themselves from the city that goes about its business at a slower pace. Elaine's compression bandage has to be removed because it has become dampened during her shower.

There is enough time after breakfast to refill the car tank, buy some items for tomorrow evening and take a stroll in the Caltech grounds. The Jurgensen building is undergoing rehabilitation and extensive changes nearly half a century since its initial construction; the campus every year is filled gradually with more buildings or extensions that have transformed the feeling of open space to one of a well-managed and well landscaped contemporary university campus.

On Green Street Malbec is still a successful and vibrant restaurant because of the quality of its food, service and prices; it is here we meet with Maria and Vicente who already secured a booth in the deeper recess of the restaurant and are looking lively but serious. Vicente's face looks more aged than I recall and quite possibly he experiences the same impression for me.

During the first part of our encounter Maria launches in a monologue with Elaine while Vicente and I exchange little information; wine loosens the tongue and he and I talk about age, risks and survival. The Pacific sole I ordered is fresh and well-prepared, food of which I enjoy each morsel while talking or thinking of the area we are in. In 1966 we came to Pasadena for the first time for a medical consultation with Dr. Starr; his office was a block away from Malbec; in 1979 there was a travel agency nearby that specialized in travel to unusual places, one which I asked to prepare an itinerary for our first trip to South America. After the owner of the agency displayed negligence and indifference I took the project to Dick's Travel in South Lake; the agency which was then official travel office for Caltech worked out an itinerary that met our wishes and they made all arrangements needed. In the early 80's we found an old walnut bed from England that became our bed for many years; the antique business was housed in the building where Dr. Starr had practiced. I shifted my mind away from these thoughts to listen to the current conversation.

...
At Domna and Arturo's place we arrive promptly at 6:00 pm, in spite of heavy traffic, to find the cheerful and recently maintained house all lit up. Friends at the door welcome us and share cheer. Rodanthi arrives soon limping slightly with a cane that might have been a wizard's wand.

Dinner at Bistro de la Gare stretches out with an informed and intelligent discussion that focuses on the economic, political and social problems of our time. We depart after the restaurant is completely empty.

Pasadena 11 November 2011

2.92

Will it rain? Overcast skies and a slight breeze betray a chance of precipitation only. In the semi-darkness of early morning I feel little inclined to rise and take a shower. There is no definite schedule until the evening except there is a list of things we must attend before this afternoon.

...
Venerable Vroman's Bookstore is a holdout in the post-paper era with strong following but declining variety in book inventory. How times change when new technology achieves a shift in paradigm; now it is the turn of the digital media.

...
South on 605 unpredictable traffic patterns and rain make driving tiring and irritating, nonetheless we arrive early at our destination where we quietly wait for ten minutes before seeing our dear friends. In the hoopla of the first few minutes I manage to unload baskets and bags of gifts from the Fruit and Nut Express with the little terrier yipping at my heels. Susi and Isabel laughing manage the dinner preparation before Val and Lia arrive. They arrive shortly, Val carrying the contrived and delicious pâtée and Lia their festive gift packages. All in all everyone

makes the most of the available time in this yearly event at the expense of giving full consideration to the meal.

The end of main course is the time of gift exchanges and more photo taking. Dessert with a glass of Warre's 1999 late vintage Oporto is followed by La Famiglia Part 2 showing in the entertainment room downstairs.

Around 1:00 am we retire for the remainder of the night to Susi's place.

Pasadena 12 November 2011

2.93

The sun is shining; I open shutters to let the light and air in. In the kitchen I prepare café filtre and toast raisin bagels while E wakes up. We leisurely breakfast and talk quietly in the brightest room of the house that faces a covered patio with flower pots and blooming bougainvillea.

Isabel and Susi arrive while I wash plates and cups from breakfast; over a glass of juice we attempt to catch up with a year's news until a visitor, good friend and former colleague drops in with a pot of exquisite orchids and birthday wishes, sharing for a while our company as his golden retriever intrudes in the terrier's territory. At noon we load up the car to return to Pasadena.

...

With the name, The Vol. 94, the new restaurant Gus and Maria have discovered and take us to what is a self-proclaimed wine bar in its fledgling stage. The eclectic menu contains French, Italian and Asian inspired small plates; the wine list is under development and the young Korean owner charming and uncertain. A huge pillar at the front of the long and tall dining room seems to have no purpose or justification, reflecting the present state of confusion in the place.

It is a pleasant experience to be able to listen to our hosts in a quiet venue and be informed of their family news and their latest large undertaking in the Leica and other collectible camera world. Vincent Bohanec now has the burden of the company he works for placed on his shoulders; Yolanda Bohanec plans a visit to Pasadena before Christmas after several years of strained family relations. Regrettably Gus and Maria have not visited their house in Baja for five years; we urge them to do their best to break the spell even for a short week.

Gigi is an old dog now but she waits for us back at home, wearing a vest and wagging her tail; she does not have the zest and mischief I still remember about her. Gus displays his work at his workshop; truly fine craftsmanship from a master of Leica and of the finest and most detailed work.

Over a cup of espresso we say our goodbye for the year to return to the hotel with thoughts of next day's return trip.

Pasadena 13 November 2011

Index

PLACES

Bhutan 1, 17, 18, 19, 20, 21, 22, 23, 24, 25, 27, 29, 30, 31, 32, 34, 35, 44, 124
Greece
  Athens 73, 75, 83, 85, 86, 87, 88, 89, 90, 91, 101, 111
  Larissa 74, 78, 81, 82, 83
  Thessaloniki 71, 72, 73, 74, 76, 77, 78
  Varimbombi 84, 85, 86
India
  Darjeeling 8, 9, 11, 12, 13, 15
  Delhi 2, 4, 5, 7, 8, 13, 34, 124
  Sikkim 8, 12, 13, 14, 15, 16
  W. Bengal 17, 19
Italy
  Sicily
    Palermo 92, 93, 94, 95, 96, 107
    Ragusa 99, 100
    Siracusa 101, 103
    Taormina 104, 105, 107
U.S.A.
  California
    Altadena 56, 60
    Fiddletown 1, 35, 36, 37, 38, 39, 40, 41, 42, 44, 45, 46, 50, 51, 52, 53, 54, 55, 65, 66, 67, 68, 69, 108, 109, 110, 111, 112, 119, 120, 121, 122, 132
    Irvine 64
    Los Angeles 29, 63, 114, 115, 126, 134
    Pasadena 56, 57, 58, 59, 60, 61, 62, 64, 113, 114, 115, 116, 117, 118, 122, 123, 124, 125, 126, 127, 128, 133, 134, 135, 136, 137, 138, 139
    San Francisco 43, 44
  Oregon
    Ashland 47, 49, 50, 130
    Portland 47, 48, 49

REFLECTIONS

Lost memories 65
Saudade 131
Time 133

REMINISCENCES

Birthday celebration 30
Festering wound 35
Illness 44
Invitation to dinner 29
Leg bruise 3
Shingles 40

YEARS

1965 75
1966 136
1979 136
1999 138
2000 48
2007 82
2008 1, 2, 5, 7, 9, 12, 14, 15, 16, 17, 19, 21, 22, 25, 27, 30, 32, 34, 35, 36
2009 36, 37, 38, 39, 40, 41, 42, 43, 44, 45, 46, 47, 48, 49, 50, 51, 52, 53, 54, 55, 56, 58, 59, 60, 61, 62, 64, 65, 66
2010 67, 68, 69, 70, 71, 72, 73, 74, 76, 77, 78, 79, 80, 81, 83, 84, 85, 86, 87, 89, 90, 91, 93, 94, 95, 96, 97, 98, 100, 101, 103, 104, 105, 107, 108, 109, 110, 111, 112, 113, 114, 116, 118, 119
2011 120, 121, 122, 123, 125, 126, 127, 128, 129, 130, 131, 132, 133, 134, 135, 137, 138, 139

Index

www.ingramcontent.com/pod-product-compliance
Lightning Source LLC
LaVergne TN
LVHW091302080426
835510LV00007B/358